STEM Through the Months

for Budding, Scientists, Engineers, Mathematicians, Makers, Poets and Artists

Winter Edition

by

Gary Carnow ■ Beverly Ellman ■ Joyce Koff

Second Edition

We are appreciative of the staff and students of the following schools for their enthusiastic participation in the making of this book:
Coeur d'Alene Elementary, Venice, CA
Grant Elementary, Santa Monica, CA
Paul Revere Middle School, Los Angeles, CA
Santa Monica High School, Santa Monica, CA

For information about Clever Thinkers and Inventive Thinkers® workshops write to:

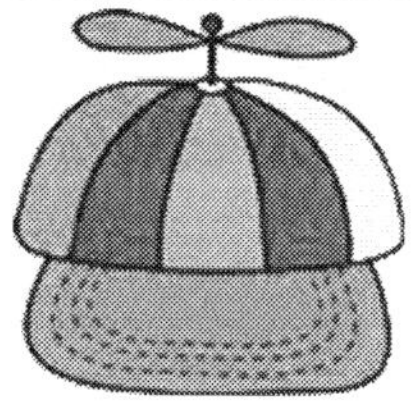

Inventive Thinkers®
www.inventivethinkers.org
inventivethinkers@gmail.com

Clever Thinkers
cleverthinkers.net
cleverthinkers@gmail.com

Some illustrations by Sian Bowman

ISBN-13: 978-1502767738
ISBN-10: 1502767732

Table of Contents

December

December – New Year's Eve Lessons and Projects

December – National Write a Friend Month Lessons and Projects

December – Winter Lessons and Projects

December – Holiday Lessons and Projects

January

January – Celebration of Life Month Lessons and Projects

January – Martin Luther King, Jr. Day Lessons and Projects

January – International Thank You Day Lessons and Projects

January – New Year's Day Lessons and Projects

February

February - National Freedom Day Lessons and Projects

February - Presidents' Day Lessons and Projects

February - Black History Month Lessons and Projects

February - Valentine's Day Lessons and Projects

WELCOME

Welcome to the Winter Edition of *STEM Through the Months for Budding Scientists, Engineers, Mathematicians, Makers and Poets.* Designed for teachers and students, these activities help you make and create wonderful classroom experiences. Using monthly-themed events as a springboard, poetry as a language arts component and the maker movement for inspiration, your students will build cross-curricular connections as they explore STEM – science, technology, engineering and mathematics.

THIS WINTER EDITION IS DESIGNED FOR YOU

This edition was designed for teachers, students and parents as a companion to the other editions in this series. The activities are primarily for students in grades three through eight. We know you will find these engaging and innovative lessons and projects easy to adopt and adapt for learners of all ages. For each special or silly day of the winter months there is a STEAM learning prompt. Need a lesson idea? Simply turn to the day of your choice and you're off and running. The projects and poetry lessons have been classroom-tested and provide enjoyable learning experiences in a variety of environments: a traditional classroom, home schooling, after-school programs, scouting, gifted and talented programs, extracurricular clubs and ESL classes. For families looking for weekend or rainy day activities, we think you will find this to be a useful resource. And for kids who thumb through the special days and holidays, we ask, what will you make?

WHAT'S INSIDE?

Inside you will find three jam-packed months of STEM lessons, projects and poetry experiences inspired by holidays, special days, traditional observances and wacky celebrations. Drawing on the inner poet in every child and the "let me do-it-myself" nature inherent in all learners, the activities and lessons will help your students earn an "A" for the Arts and will bring STEAM to your STEM initiatives. Your budding scientists, mathematicians and engineers will practice creative and inventive thinking skills as they build knowledge throughout the year. The special days and projects feature the months of December, January and February. Do not feel obliged to use these ideas and projects only in these specific months. The projects and activities are great with their calendar collaborations, but your curriculum and schedule may vary. Perhaps your class is reading a story about aviation in October and the projects presented fit at that time, let your curriculum take flight. We encourage you to use the activities and projects on a day that fits into your classroom plans.

HOW IS THE WINTER BOOK ORGANIZED?

We begin each month with monthly, weekly and movable holidays. Whether it's a silly celebration or a traditional holiday, you will find it listed here, ready to kick start the imaginations of your students. Next, Make and Do Days for STEM Makers and Poets highlight each day of the month with background information and STEM/STEAM activity starters. Featured are four units of study that coincide with special days and holidays for each month and additional extension lessons. For example, the E in STEM is for Engineering. In January we celebrate International Thank You Day and students experience assembly lines in an engineering activity. The corresponding poetry lesson featuring a poem by Ralph Waldo Emerson ties nicely with the greeting card factory line that students design and implement. Each major lesson is followed by a poetry lesson that correlates with the unit of study. Students write poems in the style of the selected poet and learn about the poet in a biography that is easily duplicated along with the poem for use in your classroom. Additional poems that enhance the unit are also included. Each month learning standards are correlated to the technology standards from the International Society for Technology in Education (ISTE, 2016); the Next Generation Science Standards (NGSS) in science and engineering; and the language arts and math Common Core State Standards Initiative.

ABOUT STEM

STEM is an acronym for four disciplines: science, technology, engineering and mathematics. These four disciplines are related and overlap, but we tend not to think of STEM as unique unto itself. STEM has become the next big thing due to concerns that U.S. students are falling behind and will not be able to fill the void left by an aging workforce. As we become increasingly global dependent, we want our students to be on a level playing field. Educators and parents have no doubt heard the STEM acronym, but are often confused as to what it means or what it actually looks like.

As classrooms adopt STEM activities, teachers and students quickly realize that design thinking and project-based learning are at the core of all STEM disciplines. To be college and career ready, a firm foundation of mathematics is required. Science is also essential and is a part of modern life. Science includes a body of knowledge and the ability to follow methods and processes to construct understanding. There are many scientific disciplines taught in school (for example, life science, earth science, physical science) and they spiral and interlap. In K-12, engineering education has long been overlooked. Engineering brings design thinking to the classroom and students collaborate, communicate, and think creatively as they construct solutions to real-world problems. The practical applications of engineering in conjunction with science and math foundations are a necessity. Technology is a part of our everyday life and should be a part of daily school practice. Technology, particularly computing technology, be it handheld devices or desktop computers, is a tool that enhances learning. Technology can be an underlying support in all aspects of schooling, not just a tool for STEM disciplines.

As STEM education is adopted in state standards for mathematics and included in the Next Generation Science Standards (NGSS), schools are looking for innovative ways to integrate these highly engaging disciplines. We believe that STEM experiences are important for all students at all grade levels. We see STEM as highly engaged learning and we know that you will find the projects and activities in this book helpful.

STEM GAINS AN "A" - STEAM

The national movement to provide STEM experiences for students gains steam on a daily basis. This is why we have focused heavily on the arts to integrate a big "A" into STEM. We know that you and your students will especially love the core poetry lessons. Students enjoy poetry and learning about famous poets and their poems integrate easily with your STEM and common core focus. Also included are several arts lessons focusing on photography, the fine arts, music and dance.

CONNECTION BETWEEN POETRY AND STEM

STEM learning and teaching encourages students to observe their world through their senses. Students construct knowledge through observation and practice in science, technology, engineering and math. This is also true for poetry. By exposure to poets, their lives and their works, students extend their observational skills as they write their own poems. And both poetry and mathematics contain patterns, rhythms and beats. Both are mysterious and need to be understood to comprehend. Then their secrets unfold. From our teaching experience, we have learned that some teachers are uncomfortable teaching poetry. You will be amazed how easily these classroom-tested activities will assist young poets in discovering the joy of writing.

Reading poetry out loud reveals a unique rhythm of sounds and beats and, in this way, poetry is immersive and experiential. Students are drawn instinctively to poetry because it allows them the freedom to use language in new and original ways. Students particularly enjoy straying from traditional grammar, capitalization and punctuation in some of their original works. Students are also intrigued by poetry that has an original visual look.

Each monthly chapter includes the work of four famous poets. Each selected poet is presented along with a biography, a sample poem and a lesson guide. Most of the poems we have selected are in the public domain. Those that are not, are easily found. Your students

will call upon their inner voices as they experience writing a poem in the style of the poet that they are studying. Students will also gain an appreciation for the life circumstances and the period of time in which the poet lived and worked. Each poet is matched with a corresponding activity for each facet of STEM (science, technology, engineering and mathematics). The poets are the glue that binds each unit of study in the book and provide a unique language arts underpinning to STEM education.

TECHNOLOGY

We hope that you have access to some classroom or school technology. As technology using educators, we know that consistent involvement with technology enriches the classroom experience. For over thirty years, students and teachers have used technology tools to add exciting dimensions and high interest to classroom work. We have specifically designed these activities and projects to be enriched through the use of technology; however, it is not a pre-requisite. Paper, pencils and other common classroom supplies will suffice. If you have access to a few computers and a printer, great; we believe strongly in using what you have. There is no need to go out and buy the latest and greatest.

Handhelds including tablets, smartphones, watches and other devices utilize mobile apps that can enhance your learning environment. Students become engaged in their learning and build knowledge through hands-on experiences with various apps. Some schools have adopted BYOD (bring your own device) policies that enrich their technology opportunities for their students. You don't need a full classroom set of anything to integrate technology into your curriculum.

Many schools have employed Chromebooks for use in their classrooms. With a Chromebook, students use Google Docs, Sheets and Slides as their productivity applications. Google also provides Chromebook Classroom, Picasa, Calendar, and Sites. New features and applications are enhanced and added on a regular basis. Third-party developers have also created essential tools and fun applications. With a Chromebook, students create their documents and presentations and store them in the cloud using Google Drive. Students can invite others to collaborate on their documents giving them the ability to edit, view and comment. You can also view a document's revision history and go back to previous versions. Google Docs plays well with Microsoft Word, OpenOffice, Pages and other word processing programs. Similarly, Google Sheets imports and converts from Excel and other spreadsheet file formats, including Numbers. Google Slides share formats with PowerPoint and Keynote.

Many of the projects in this book use word processing, spreadsheet and presentation software. Whether you have access to computers with that software on the drive or Chromebooks with the application in the cloud, you are set to go. For classrooms with laptops or desktop computers with a hard drive, you have the additional functionality of editing video and using music software. Many tablets and iPads with apps like iMovie and Garage Band will also give you this functionality.

TECHNOLOGY TOOLS AND APPS

Here are a few of our favorite technology tools and apps, divided into a series of categories. Programs come and go. What was initially free, may now be a paid app or require a subscription. In any event, hopefully you will find something new to try with some of our favorites.

Art, Graphics and Photo Software

Blender (free and open source) - https://www.blender.org/
Corel Paint Shop
Kid Pix Deluxe 4 and Kid Pix 3D
Photoshop and Photoshop Elements
PIXLR (free) – https://pixlr.com
Turtle Art (free) – http://turtleart.org
Tux Paint (free) – http://tuxpaint.org
wpclipart (public domain clip art for schoolkids) - https://www.wpclipart.com/index.html

Education Suites

Adobe Creative Cloud (monthly subscription)
Apple Keynote, Numbers, and Pages (bundled with a Mac)
Google Apps (Classroom, Gmail, Drive, Calendar, Docs, Sheets, Slides, and Sites)
Microsoft Office Suite
Open Office (free) – http://openofficefreedownload.org

Design

Canva – https://www.canva.com/
PrintShop 3 for Mac – -https://www.mackiev.com/printshop3/features/whatsnew.html

Interactive Applications

HyperStudio – http://www.mackiev.com/hyperstudio/
ThingLink – https://www.thinglink.com/

iPhone/iPad/Android Apps

Snapseed – available on iTunes or Google Play
Sock Puppets – https://itunes.apple.com/us/app/sock-puppets/id394504903?mt=8
Zoodle Comics – https://itunes.apple.com/us/app/zoodle-comics/id520954201?mt=8

Miscellaneous Applications

Chartgo (free) – http://www.chartgo.com/
Create A Graph (free) - https://nces.ed.gov/nceskids/createagraph/
Comic Life - https://plasq.com/apps/comiclife/macwin/
GarageBand (bundled with a Mac)
Timeliner – http://teacher.scholastic.com/products/tomsnyder.htm

Presentation (also see Screencasting)

Any of the education suites.
PowToon (basic version free) – https://www.powtoon.com/
Prezi (free trial available) – https://prezi.com/

Programming/Coding

Scratch (free) – https://scratch.mit.edu/
Tynker (free version available, subscription plans too) – https://www.tynker.com/
Hopscotch (free) – https://www.gethopscotch.com/
Tickle (free) – https://tickleapp.com/

Screencasting Tools

Snagit – https://www.techsmith.com/snagit.html
Screencast-O-Matic – https://screencast-o-matic.com/home
Screencastify – https://www.screencastify.com/
Movenote – https://www.movenote.com/
Explain Everything – http://explaineverything.com/

Search Engines

Duck Duck Go (free) – https://duckduckgo.com/
Google
Google Kiddle (free) – http://www.kiddle.co/

Video Editing

Adobe Premiere Elements
Adobe Premiere Pro (subscription)
Animoto (free trial available) – https://animoto.com/
iMovie (free with Mac purchase)
Loopster (web based, basic version free) – http://www.loopster.com/
WeVideo (web based, free trial available) – https://www.wevideo.com/

Writing

Inspiration, Kidspiration and Kidspiration Maps (lite version free) – http://www.inspiration.com/
Stationery Studio Writing Collection Deluxe – http://shop.fablevisionlearning.com
Storybird – https://storybird.com/

CLASSROOM PUBLISHING

STEM activities and projects come to life through the study and practice of language arts. The International Council of Teachers of English has identified five strands of language arts – reading, writing, speaking, listening and viewing (visual literacy). Students use language arts to show others their thinking, compositions and creativity. Making work public validates the work. As early as the one-room schoolhouse, teachers have displayed student writing and drawings. Work was sent home and no doubt published on refrigerator doors in the 1930s.

With appropriate technology your students can discover, invent and explore as they publish, illustrate and arrange their written work. These *STEM Through The Months* projects and lessons will be enhanced if you have access to word processing software or classroom publishing software. Your students will enrich their STEM content as they also develop skills in page layout, illustrations, color and typography. Students will also receive value from seeing their ideas in print, whether they are working on a report or a classroom newsletter. We encourage you to explore the use of a simple digital handheld device, for example, a camera or a tablet, so that students can publish their work to digital lockers, websites or social media.

"STEM'ING" ACROSS THE CURRICULUM

You may be familiar with "writing across the curriculum." Today we challenge you to use "STEM'ing" across the curriculum. The activities in this book follow monthly, weekly and daily celebrations across the academic spectrum, including English language arts, mathematics, science, social studies, fine arts, performing arts, and health. STEM learners work in a student-centered learning environment. Their participation is continuously encouraged through questioning, problem solving, collaboration and hands-on activities. Teacher facilitators guide students as they plan and design projects and work in groups to apply the rigors of science, technology, engineering and mathematics contents to achieve their goals.

COMPUTER PROGRAMMING

Schools are looking at ways to add programming into their curriculum. The tools to do so are readily available and even young children are learning to code. Most of the readily available block programming languages are related to Seymour Papert's Logo. Logo is more than just a programming language, it is also a philosophy of education. Logo employs discovery learning and is linked with constructivism, a learning theory. Constructivism relies on students experimenting and solving real-world problems. Students construct their knowledge and understanding through experiences and reflective thought.

A good place to get started is with Scratch, designed for kids at the MIT Media Lab. Scratch is browser-based and is on the web. There are millions of projects created and ready for you to explore, remix and customize to your liking. There are plenty of tutorials and educator websites for you to explore. Get started here at https://scratch.mit.edu/. Scratch works well with many of the projects in this book. Presentations and animations can be done in Scratch.

WHAT IS THE MAKER MOVEMENT?

The Maker Movement is a revolutionary global collaboration of people learning to solve problems with modern tools and technology. Children and adults are combining new technologies and timeless craft traditions to create exciting projects. The Maker and DIY (Do-It-Yourself) movements are fostering a new enthusiasm to work with your hands and see tangible results. In the 1990s, as we prepared a new generation of knowledge workers, the goal was to round up all warm bodies and send them off to college, then to a cubicle in a career to fuel the information economy. This vision has not materialized. Now, more than ever, we need people who know how to do things: build houses, fix cars and solve problems.

WHAT IS A MAKERSPACE?

The new buzz word is makerspace. These spaces are sometimes called STEM Labs, STEAM Labs and/or Fab Labs. As the Maker Movement continues to grow exponentially in local communities, makers in on-line spaces and physical spaces are coming together in meet-ups and hackerspaces to create, collaborate and share resources. These spaces are what we call makerspaces. They come in many shapes and sizes. Students use makerspaces to build and invent as they creatively engage. A makerspace is more than an art room, a woodshop, a computer lab or a science lab. A makerspace, however, may contain elements found in these traditional spaces.

A makerspace culture promotes student construction and prototyping. Students cross-pollinate their ideas and knowledge as they make products and solve problems. These activity hubs foster collaboration and a culture of creativity. The activities support design thinking, project-based learning and STEM/STEAM initiatives.

We encourage you to start with what you have. Your space might be a mini-space or a pop-up space. Your makerspace may initially, double as another space. Don't worry too much about the physical space, what is more important is the building of a maker and design thinking culture. A makerspace is not necessarily defined by what tools and materials are contained in the space, but is perhaps better defined by what happens in the space – *making*

WHAT GOES IN A MAKERSPACE?

Making is not a shopping list of products. With that said, there are categories of maker materials and tools that you may wish to consider.

- Arts and Crafts
  Materials (cardboard, paint, felt, etc.)
  Tools (glue gun, a Cricut®, silk screen, etc.)

- Building Systems
  Erector Sets®
  LEGO®
  K'NEX®
  Lincoln Logs®
  Tinkertoys®

- Computer Controlled Fabrication
  Additive Fabrication (3D printers)
  Subtractive Fabrication (mills, cutters)

- Computers
  Chromebooks
  Desktops
  iPhones and Android phones
  Laptops
  Tablets
  Watches

- Conductive Materials
  Traditional – wire, solder, brads, paper clips
  New – conductive thread, yarn, paint, fabric, yarn, graphite
  Future – electro conductive adhesive gel (Tac Gel) and biomaterials

- Electronics
  Batteries
  Displays
  LEDs
  Motors
  Sensors

- Interfaces
  MaKey MaKey
  Hummingbird

- Physical Computing
  Microcontrollers (Arduino, HyperDuino)
  Microcomputers (RaspberryPi)
  Robotics

- Programming
  Block programming (Scratch, SNAP)
  Text-based programming (C++, Python, Arduino)

- Textiles and Sewing
  e-textiles
  Wearables (Arduino, Lilypad, Flora)

MAKER TOOLS AND RESOURCES

Many of the lessons and projects in this book can be enhanced with maker tools and resources. The units and lesson extensions are starting points that can be enhanced with some of the exciting maker products now available. There are a variety of low-cost products that work with a computer and will challenge your students. Here are just a few of the many creative, open-ended products that your students can use to enhance your STEM/STEM curriculum with maker experiences. There is a growing list of materials and kits chock full of creative projects to try. Search Google for maker materials and supplies and you will find a wealth of choices. For example:

- littleBits – http://littlebits.cc/
  littleBits has a library of over sixty modules and each module works with every other. They begin with a power source, like a battery, and snap together (with magnets) to create a circuit. It's an easy way to learn how electronics work with or without programming skills. There is no soldering or use of breadboards. You can control the input and output with touch sensors and wires to create motion, light lights and create sounds. littleBits however, is not low-cost.

- MaKey Makey - http://www.makeymakey.com/
  MaKey MaKey is an invention kit. You turn everyday objects into touchpads and combine them with the Internet. The kit comes with an interface board, alligator clips, a USB cable and instructions. You can use any material that will conduct a bit of electricity to send your computer a keyboard or mouse input. Kids can become artists, engineers and designers as they create projects. They can devise games, mazes, musical instruments and much more.

- Makedo - https://mymakedo.com/
  Makedo are tools for cardboard construction. Using recycled cardboard you can build anything. If you can dream it, you can build it. Makedo are simple plastic parts, a safe-saw, plastic "scrus" and straps that become joints or hinges. Your projects will promote collaboration and problem solving.

- Hummingbird – www.humingbirdkit.com
  The Hummingbird Robotics Kit is a product of the Carnegie Mellon's CREATE Lab. Hummingbird's enable robotic and engineering activities. It is aimed at ages thirteen and up, but works well with ages eight and up with adult supervision. The kit parts along with crafting materials can make robots, animatronics and kinetic sculptures. Hummingbirds play well with Scratch and other programming languages.

- HyperDuino – www.hyperduino.com
  HyperDuino enables you to easily create your own interactive maker projects. The HyperDuino is a piggy-back board to an Arduino (a microcontroller) that connects to a Chromebook, a Macintosh and/or a Windows computer. The two-way hyperlink connects models in the physical world to the microcontroller. For example, you program the controller to play a video segment on a computer or light an LED on your physical model.

3D PRINTING

In this book there are many projects where you could incorporate a 3D printer and use the products you make in some of the activities. Besides the obvious technology and engineering aspects of 3D printing, students can design and prototype projects in a way they could have never done before. Kids have made musical instruments, jewelry and scale models of buildings and monuments and so much more.

Home hobbyists have enthusiastically used 3D printers to make and create a variety of prototypes and products and now your students can too. The cost of 3D printing has dramatically decreased and schools are beginning to purchase and use 3D printers. There are a variety of printers available and more are being introduced each year. Make magazine has an annual review of these printers. Currently, printers for schools and for home use cost anywhere from $400 to $2800.

What are kids doing with a 3D printer? Kids are using computer-aided design programs to create files in the needed stereolithography file format known as .stl. These files are loaded into a 3D printer from a computer. The software that comes with the printer slices these files into layers. The printer begins the additive process of printing an object, layer by layer.

There are many websites where you can get 3D .stl files. Some of these sites feature open source files, which let you modify and customize the files to your liking. You can get an idea of what is available by visiting sites like YouMagine (www.youmagine.com) and Thingiverse (www.thingiverse.com).

NOW LET'S GET STARTED

We think you will find the lessons and projects wonderful additions to your curriculum. We know that *STEM Through the Months for Budding Scientists, Engineers, Mathematicians, Makers and Poets, Winter Edition* will jumpstart you to make, do and enjoy the winter months.

December Monthly Holidays

Art and Architecture Books Month • Bingo's Birthday Month • Hi Neighbor Month • Made in America Month • National Stress-Free Family Holiday Month • Read a New Book Month • Safe Toys and Gifts Month • Universal Human Rights Month • Winter Month

December Weekly Holidays

First Week of December
Christmas Tree Week

Second Week of December
Civil Rights Week • Human Rights Week • National Drunk Drivers Awareness Week

Third Week of December
International Language Week • Tell Someone They're Doing a Good Job Week

Last Week of December
Kwanzaa begins on December 26 • National Game and Puzzle Week • Orange Bowl Week

December Moveable Holidays

Apple Pie Day .... Thursday after first Tuesday

Army and Navy Union Day... second Saturday

Klopfeinachte ....three Thursdays before Christmas

Election Day .... first Tuesday after the first Monday

Kiwi Day.. first day of Winter

Underdog Day... third Friday

December Days for STEM Makers and Poets

Science Technology Engineering Arts Math

		Day	Make and Do
1		Rosa Parks Day	On this day in 1955 Rosa Parks refused to give up her seat on a bus in Montgomery, Alabama. She was arrested for violating Alabama's segregation laws. The United States Congress has said that Mrs. Parks was "the first lady of civil rights" and "the mother of the freedom movement." Today we honor her memory and ask ourselves how could we make the world a better place? Write your ideas as a poem or a story.
2		National Mutt Day	Mixed breed dogs desperately await new homes. Celebrate and help awareness about the millions of loving mutts living in shelters. Mixed breed dogs are just as able to perform the duties of purebred dogs. Make a list of seven things you can do to help and use one of your ideas in a National Mutt Day poster. Create the poster with your favorite page design program.
3		Make a Gift Day	Makers love to make and there is nothing better than giving a homemade gift. For Make a Gift Day, design and craft a gift. Pinterest is a great site for ideas for the DIY (Do-It-Yourself) maker and crafter. Why not create a "Make Your Own Puppet" kit? Take a cellophane bag and fill it with craft materials and a small bottle of glue. Design your own label and staple it across the top. Your friends will love your very creative gift.

4		National Cookie Day	Holiday season is definitely cookie season. Who doesn't like cookies? For those of you who like to bake cookies, learn why baking cookies is both an art and a science. What is the science behind baking cookies? For example, recipes with more butter give you thinner and crisper cookies and if you use baking powder rather than baking soda you get softer cookies. Melted butter and bread flour makes a chewier cookie. Why is this so? Search the web for a favorite cookie recipe for the best cookie ever. Word process the recipe onto a 4 x 6 recipe card.
5		International Volunteer Day	Established by the General Assembly of the United Nations in 1985, we celebrate volunteers from community groups, non-profits and the private sector. Make a difference by helping others. Find causes you are interested in and want to learn about. Become an environmental engineer. What project would you like to see completed in your community? Develop and implement a work plan. Write or blog about your experience.
6		St. Nicholas Day	Today is a festival day in many European countries celebrating the legends of Saint Nicholas known for bringing gifts. British Father Christmas and the American Santa Claus are both similarly derived. Share the St. Nicholas you know. Work with a partner to create a slide as part of a class slide show. Consider using KidPix, HyperStudio, Keynote or PowerPoint. Include stories, songs and pictures.
7		Pearl Harbor Remembrance Day	The attack on Pearl Harbor brought America into World War II in the Pacific. Look up newspaper headlines from that day and create a three column newspaper with a headline, photo and text in a desktop publishing software program.

8		National Brownie Day	Find a really fudgy brownie recipe and create a shopping list. What will it cost to make your brownies? Create a spreadsheet to determine how much it will cost to make one brownie. How much will it cost to make enough brownies for your class? For your entire school?
9		Christmas Card Day	The first Christmas card was printed and sent in England in 1843. For makers and DIY'ers, engineer a pop-up holiday card. Use the web to research how to make your card. You will find great ideas and examples with video and step-by-step directions. Begin your search at www.wikihow.com.
10		Nobel Prize Day	Alfred Nobel signed his last will and testament giving a large share of his fortune to prizes in Chemistry, Literature, Medicine, Physics and Peace. The official website of the Nobel Prize is www.nobelprize.org. Here you will find a world of activities and resources. Learn about one of the Nobel Prize winners. On Nobel Prize Day, present your prizewinner as a poster or a slide.
11		UNICEF's Birthday	UNICEF was founded to help children after World War II. UNICEF's mission is for "a better world for children everywhere." For resources including topics by grade and by media, go to TeachUNICEF.org. Create a one-minute Public Service Announcement (PSA) highlighting one of UNICEF's programs. Find inspiring recent Youth Video Contest winners at: http://www.unicef.org/videoaudio//video_videocontest.html

unicef

12		Gingerbread House Day	Calling all engineers! Get your creativity on and build a gingerbread house. Download house patterns, recipes and templates or watch videos on the web. Once you are familiar with what it takes, design your own masterpiece. Build a cardboard model of your house to use as a pattern for the gingerbread. Find a recipe on the web. Gingerbread is usually comprised mostly of flour, baking soda and dark molasses along with ginger, cinnamon, nutmeg, cloves, sugar, salt, eggs and shortening. Cut the rolled out dough into the shapes of your template and bake. Royal Icing glues it all together. Decorate your house with candy.
13		Ban a Silly Superstition Day	What is the silliest superstition that you know? Design an ad campaign to ban that superstition. Layout your plan in a presentation program.
14		Monkey Day	It's Monkey Day and what can be more fun than a barrel of monkeys? How about a monkey that can paint like Andy Warhol? Our fellow primates can learn to paint with their tails. Let's try some monkey tail art by braiding heavy yarn, dipping it in paint, and using the braid as your brush to paint like a monkey.
15		Bill of Rights Day	The first ten amendments to the United States Constitution are collectively known as the Bill of Rights. These rights prohibit governmental powers from taking away an individual's liberties. Your class may already have class rules. This is a great day to discuss individual rights and responsibilities. Create a two-column chart of ten classroom rights you have and ten corresponding classroom responsibilities. For example, you have the right to be treated with respect and the responsibility to treat others with respect.

16		National Chocolate Covered Anything Day	Calling all chocoholics! Today is your day to cover everything you eat in chocolate. It's also an excellent day to learn about the various kinds of chocolate: bittersweet, semisweet, milk, white, dark, sweetened, unsweetened and more. Research the history of chocolate beginning with the Cacao bean. Aztecs and Mayans used the valuable beans as currency. Become a product engineer. What would you like to dip in chocolate? What is the most outrageous chocolate-covered treat that you can think of? Name your creation and create the packaging for your product.
17		Wright Brother's Day	American brothers, Orville and Wilbur took to the air on this day in 1903, ushered in the age of flying machines. Their imaginations were sparked by a childhood toy helicopter. In honor of the innovative brothers, make a few different paper helicopters. You will find templates on the web. What design works best? Decide which design spins the longest or falls to the ground the slowest.
18		Pantomime Day	Pantomime is a theatrical entertainment performed around the winter holidays. Joseph Grimaldi, a famous English actor, comedian and dancer known for pantomime was born on this day in 1778. Pantomime is aimed at children and involves slapstick comedy, music and topical jokes often based on a fairy tale or a nursery story. In a group, create a five minute pantomime extravaganza.
19		National Hard Candy Day	How do you make hard candy? Find a basic recipe and adapt it with your own special ingredients. Write out your recipe. How much of each ingredient will you need? How much will you need of each ingredient to make enough hard candy for everyone in your class to have three pieces?

20		This Day in History	The Louisiana Purchase was completed on this day in 1803. How much did it cost? What could you purchase with that amount of money today?
21		Crossword Puzzle Day	Are you a cruciverbalist, a person who is skillful in creating or solving crossword puzzles? Arthur Wynne's puzzle was published in a New York Sunday newspaper in 1913. Other newspapers discovered this pastime and crosswords became featured in almost all American newspapers. Create a winter crossword puzzle. Make a list of winter words. Build your puzzle using an online crossword puzzle builder. One site, Instant Online Crossword Puzzle Maker, is found at http://www.puzzle-maker.com/CW/.
22		International Arbor Day	Learn the eight landscape features to take into consideration when planting a tree at the Arbor Day Foundation website. Create a sketchbook of trees in your neighborhood and start a tree from a seedling.
23		Roots Day	Celebrate your heritage on Roots Day. Many people return home for the holidays and enjoy the cozy sense of belonging. Your celebrations may include traditional foods and family customs. Create a Roots Day booklet about your family, either with pen and paper or in a multimedia program. Consider including some family photos with recordings of family members talking about your family's roots.
24		Christmas Eve Broadcast	The U.S. Navy had only heard Morris Code coming over the airways. But on Christmas Eve in 1906 this changed. Alerted to listen for a special message at 9 PM they suddenly heard the human voice of Reginald Fessenden over their headphones, followed by singing and a violin solo. Imagine hearing the first radio broadcast and how exciting that must have been. How would you spend Christmas Eve with just a radio? Plan, make and record your own holiday radio show podcast.

25		A'Phabet Day or No "L" Day	Say "Noel" out loud and you will understand the pun intended for A'Phabet Day. Celebrate the day by not speaking or texting without the use of the letter "L". Make a list of twenty-five words you "a'tered".
26		Boxing Day	Boxing Day follows Christmas Day and in England and other British Commonwealth countries, tradespeople and servants received a gift known as a Christmas Box. This practice may date back to the Middle Ages. Examine a box to determine its height, width and depth. Determine the number of cubic units the box will hold. Compare the sizes of several boxes.
27		Visit the Zoo Day	Visit your local zoo or visit the National Zoo online at http://nationalzoo.si.edu/. Using the presentation software of your choice, create a Zoo Tour Book with video clips, sounds, stories or poems.
28		Pledge of Allegiance Day	Written in 1892, the pledge was first recited by presidential proclamation, in public schools on Columbus Day. The modern version was approved by Congress in 1942. There have been four changes to the pledge with the most recent change in 1954. Research the pledge, learn about its history and determine the changes. Working with a partner, take each phrase of the pledge and create a guide to the pledge. For example, the first phrase "I pledge" could be explained by defining a pledge as a promise. When you pledge, it means you promise you are going to do something. Combine the various phrase explanations into a class book, physically or virtually.
29		Tick Tock Day	The clock is ticking and you have two days left in the year to finish what you set out to do. Everyone loves the nursery rhyme Hickory Dickory Dock, so take out a pencil and paper and rewrite the rhyme with your own words. Will a mouse run up your clock?

30		Bicarbonate of Soda Day	Used for thousands of years, you may know it as baking soda, bread soda, cooking soda or bicarbonate of soda. Baking soda helps bread rise but has many other uses. For example, bicarbonate of soda can be used as a cleaning agent, as toothpaste, as an odor remover, or as a silverware polish, just to name a few uses. For budding scientists who want to see what happens when you mix an acid (vinegar) with a base (baking soda), make your own volcano.
31		New Year's Eve	New Year's Eve traditions vary from country to country. For example, in Mexico and Spain, people eat a grape for each chime on a clock's bell as they make a wish. In Copenhagen, Denmark, people gather in Radhuspladsen Town Hall Square and watch the Royal Guard parade in their uniforms and watch fireworks at the stroke of midnight. In Vienna, Austria, people gather in the streets and dance to the Blue Danube Waltz. Divide into groups and create a class book of New Year traditions around the world.

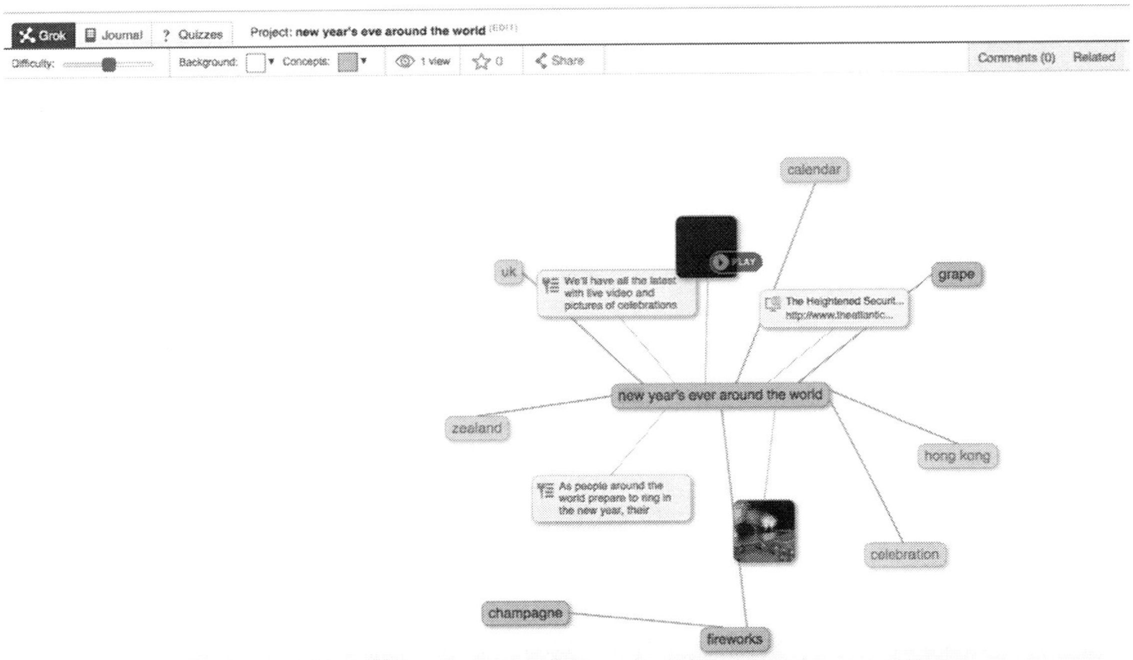

New Year's Eve Interactive Concept Map
www.instagrok.com

December Overview

New Year's Eve
Science Lesson: One Minute Drop
Poetry Lesson: A Song for New Year's Eve
by William Cullen Bryant
On New Year's Eve in 1907, the first crystal ball was dropped in New York's Times Square. Students manipulate the air resistance and drag on a dropped object to replicate this famous tradition. Two correlated poetry lessons help students reflect on the previous year and look forward to the year ahead.

National Write a Friend Month
Technology Lesson: Stationery Design
Poetry Lesson: O! why was I born with a different face?
by William Blake
We celebrate this month by encouraging children to focus on the art of hand-written letter writing. In this thematic unit, students practice the art of written correspondence, create their own computer-designed stationery, learn about acids and bases as they explore invisible ink, write a poetic letter to a friend and create crayon resist artwork.

Winter
Engineering Lesson: How to Make a Soap Carving
Poetry Lesson: Winter Haikus by Matsuo Basho
Winter, the coldest and most festive season of the year evokes a wide array of images – fireplaces, snow, rain, grey skies and freezing weather. The thematic winter unit explores engineering concepts, festive holidays, winter poetry and includes art experiences.

Holidays
Math Lesson: Shopping for Holiday Parties
Poetry Lesson: little tree by e. e. cummings
When we think of December, we think of holidays. All around the world, this is the month for celebrating Christmas, Chanukah, Kwanzaa, St. Lucia Day, New Year's Eve and more. Students practice math skills as they plan a holiday party, engineer a gum drop bridge, and write holiday poems.

Science Lesson for New Year's Eve: One-Minute Drop

New Year's Eve is celebrated all around the world. The most famous United States' celebration takes place in Times Square in New York City where the ball begins its descent at one minute before midnight and is slowly lowered down a pole. It reaches the bottom of the pole at exactly midnight, one minute later.

Students experience how air resistance or drag slows the descent of a selected object from a determined height. The goal is to see how close students come to achieving the one-minute drop of the New Year's Ball. They need to think outside the box to keep the object from falling too quickly or too slowly.

MATERIALS

Select some items below to distribute to each group.

- Paper of various weights and sizes
- Sandpaper, paper napkins, paper towels, plastic bags and more
- Heavy string, thread or yarn
- Rulers, scissors, paper clips, pencils with erasers, hole punches
- Small balls of various weights, for example, a ping pong, a golf ball, etc.
- A lightweight object, for example, a small toy, a piece of cork, a plastic spool, a chess piece
- Timers or stopwatches

PLAN

- Students work in groups to figure out how to control air resistance or drag of an item they drop. Their goal is to mimic the New York ball drop by having their objects take as close to one minute from the time it is dropped to the time it hits the ground.
- Pairs of student volunteers demonstrate the following techniques that control air resistance using a timer to measure an increase in resistance throughout the demonstration.
- First pair drops an object and times the drop.
- Continue with new pairs to demonstrate each step below. Discuss the results after each step.
  - Find parts on the object that can be removed to decrease its weight. Drop the object and time the drop.
  - Decrease the smoothness of the object. Some ways would be to crumple paper or use sand paper to scratch the surface of a plastic toy. Drop the object and time the drop.
  - Increase the size of the object. Examples would be dropping a larger sheet of paper or adding something to the object being dropped to decrease its aerodynamics. Drop the object and time the drop.
  - Create a simple parachute by attaching string to four corners of a paper item and tie the strings together around the object. Drop the object and time the drop.
  - Try other ways to slow down the object by blowing on it or adding obstacles to its path, Drop the object and time the drop.

DO

- Divide the class into small groups of five or six.
- Have students decide what materials they will use and from what height they will begin (standing on a table, chair, etc.) to achieve a one-minute drop.
- Using a timer, students continue to use air resistance techniques they have learned to come closer and closer to the one-minute goal.
- Stop once or twice while students are working to have different groups discuss and demonstrate their progress.
- At the end of the lesson have each group drop their finished object.
- As the projects are dropped, students use their timers to see how successfully each project achieved a one-minute drop.

Math Extension for New Year's Eve: Minute to Win It

On New Year's Eve in New York City, millions of people gather in Times Square to watch the New Year's Ball take its sixty-second drop to illuminate the final minute of the year. What started in New York City has been copied around the country. Each part of the country puts its own stamp on the tradition. The city of Atlanta, Georgia drops a giant peach and Miami, Florida drops Mr. Neon, a giant orange. Instead of dropping an object, the city of Seattle, Washington raises the elevator to the Space Needle; when the elevator reaches the top at exactly midnight a fireworks display illuminates the sky.

This lesson focuses on the one-minute time frame. Students discuss experiences they have had in the sixty seconds before midnight on New Years Eve. They do exercises to evaluate their ability to judge how long a minute feels. They work in small groups to try to finish a math-based Minute to Win It game. After trying out a teacher-designed game, the groups work together to create math-focused Minute to Win It games.

MATERIALS

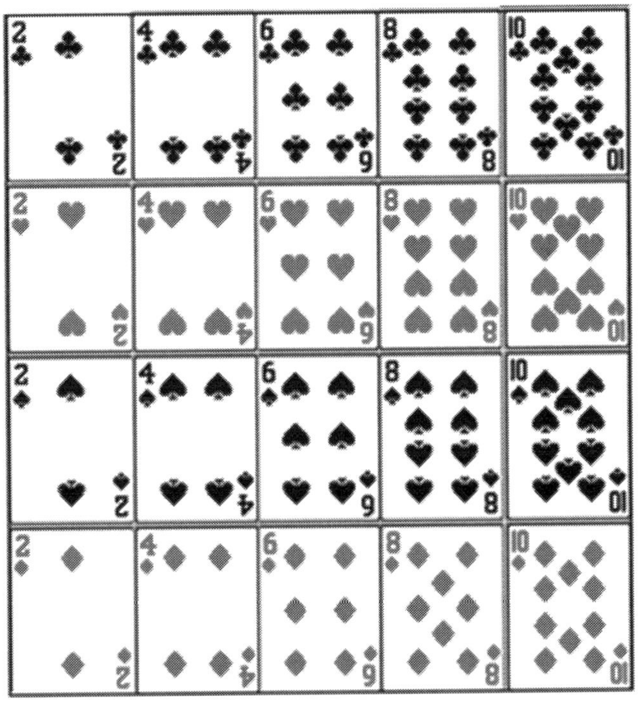

- A Minute to Win It Planning Sheet
- Commonly found objects for game play. The following list includes some suggested commonly found objects that could be gathered for use in game play:
  - Stopwatches
  - Scissors
  - Popsicle sticks
  - Markers
  - Dice
  - Decks of cards
  - Clothes pins
  - Ping pong balls
  - Paper or plastic cups
  - Paper plates
  - Hershey Kisses
  - Small candies (like M&M's)
  - Straws
  - Poster Board
  - Bowl
  - Tweezers

PLAN

- Discuss the famous New Year's Eve Ball Drop in New York City. Have students who have witnessed the drop in person and those who have watched it on television share their experiences. Expand the discussion to include other New Years Eve countdowns.
  - Have everyone stand and turn toward the back of the room.
  - Tell them you are going to set a stopwatch for sixty seconds.
  - When they think a minute has passed have them quietly face the front on the room.
  - At the end of the minute have students evaluate how close they came to judging the length of a minute.
- Divide the class into small groups and have each group repeat the above activity using stopwatches to time each other. Allow time for them to take several turns to make them better able to judge the length of a minute.
- Distribute a deck of cards to each group. Tell them their challenge is to pull the even numbers from the deck to make a new deck with all even numbers. This can be modified depending on math level to all numbers divisible by 2, divisible by 3, and so on. Have them place the cards in each group in numerical order. For example, one stack would include the 2, 4, 6, 8 and 10 of hearts. The spades, diamonds and clubs would be placed in the same order.
- Have the groups discuss whether this game was possible in a minute or whether they had had too much time left over.

DO

Have each group create A Minute to Win It Math Challenge for the class by doing the following:

- Complete the A Minute to Win It Planning Sheet.
- Gather supplies.
- Try the challenge using stopwatches to time each other and adjust the activity if it seems too easy or too difficult to complete in one minute.
- Present their challenge to the class and select volunteers to try to complete their challenge in a minute.

Taya
5th grade

Materials

Game Directions

Poetry Lesson for New Year's Eve: A Song for New Year's Eve

In his poem *A Song for New Year's Eve,* William Cullen Bryant speaks to the passing year and to his friends asking them both to stay just "one little hour, and then away." In this hour, he also asks his friends to look back at the passing year "While yet he was our guest/How cheerfully the week was spent!"

MATERIALS

- William Cullen Bryant Biography and his poem *A Song for New Year's Eve*
- Word processing or desktop publishing software or pencils, pens and paper

PLAN

- Read and discuss William Cullen Bryant's biography and poem.
- Ask the following questions:
  - To whom was Bryant speaking?
  - How did Bryant feel about the old year leaving and why did he feel that way?
  - Where does Bryant use personification when writing about the passing year?

DO

Getting Ready to Write

Ask students the following questions. As the class gives their responses, encourage discussion.

- How do you feel about your old year leaving? Why?
- Personify the New Year. What would you say to the passing year?

Writing the Poem

Using *A Song for New Year's Eve* as a model, have students write poems of their own.

- Students write poems by addressing the passing year with either "stay" for the things they liked or "away" for the things they didn't.
- Students begin each stanza with either "stay" or "away."
- Students continue their poems telling the New Year what they liked or disliked about it using personification as much as possible.

Editing and Publishing

- Students read and edit poems with partners.
- Students write their poems in a poetry book, or enter them in a word processing program and illustrate their final masterpiece.

Poet for New Year's Eve
William Cullen Bryant Biography
November 3, 1794 - June 12, 1878

William Cullen Bryant was born in Massachusetts. His mother's family came to America on the Mayflower. His father was a physician who strongly influenced William.

William learned poetry at a young age in his father's large library. One poet who had a great deal of influence on him was William Wordsworth. His father encouraged William's writing and at times even sent his poems to magazines for publication without his knowledge. At the age of ten, William had his first poem published. At thirteen his first book was published. He loved nature and like William Wordsworth celebrated it in his poems.

Although his first love was poetry, the life of a poet was not practical for him. With the encouragement of his father he became a lawyer. Eventually he left law and moved his family to New York City. There he began his career in journalism. As editor-in-chief of the Evening Post, one of the nation's most respected newspapers, he wrote articles that defended Abraham Lincoln, human rights, free trade and the abolition of slavery. Although he was also known as a poet and critic, he felt that he didn't have enough time to devote to his writing because he traveled frequently and was busy in his work as a journalist.

He didn't publish many poems in his lifetime, but he was very popular due to his writing as a journalist and his many public speeches. Bryant was one of the founders of the Republican Party, and at one time he considered running for President of the United States.

A Song for New Year's Eve
by William Cullen Bryant

Stay yet, my friends, a moment stay,
Stay till the good old year,
So long companion of our way,
Shakes hands, and leaves us here.
Oh stay, oh stay,
One little hour, and then away.

The year, whose hopes were high and strong,
Has now no hopes to wake;
Yet one hour more of jest and song
For his familiar sake.
Oh stay, oh stay,
One mirthful hour, and then away.

The kindly year, his liberal hands
Have lavished all his store.
And shall we turn from where he stands,
Because he gives no more?
Oh stay, oh stay,
One grateful hour, and then away.

Days brightly came and calmly went,
While yet he was our guest;
How cheerfully the week was spent!
How sweet the seventh day's rest!
Oh stay, oh stay,
One golden hour, and then away.

Dear friends were with us, some who sleep
Beneath the coffin-lid:
What pleasant memories we keep
Of all they said and did!
Oh stay, oh stay,
One tender hour, and then away.

Even while we sing, he smiles his last,
And leaves our sphere behind.
The good old year is with the past;
Oh be the new as kind!
Oh stay, oh stay,
One parting strain, and then away.

Poetry Lesson for New Year's Eve: Auld Lang Syne

Auld Lang Syne by Robert Burns is a universally famous song. *Auld Lang Syne* is sung on New Year's Eve at the stroke of midnight as people around the world toast to old times. Auld Lang Syne means as times go by. Burns wrote that he heard an old man singing it and copied down the words. Burns was known to change and improve old songs that he collected from fragments of ballads so he probably was responsible for the lyrics for most of the song as we know it today. In this lesson, students write a toast to old times, to a person, and to events associated with that person.

MATERIALS

- Robert Burns Biography and his poem in Scot's verse *Auld Lang Syne* and English verse *Good Ole Times*
- Word processing or desktop publishing software or pencils, pens and paper

PLAN

- Read and discuss the biography of Robert Burns with the class. Explain to students that the original song poem Burns wrote was in the Scot dialect. Discuss the meaning of dialect – a specific form of language that is particular to a region or social group.
- Ask students the following questions:
  - What does Burns mean when he asks: "Should old acquaintance be forgot and never brought to mind?"
  - What experiences is Burns toasting to that he shared with his friend?

DO

Getting Ready to Write

Ask students what important memories they have with either a friend or a family member. For example: *when we two walked on the beach and found shells, when we two sat at dinner laughing at a moment, when we two said the same thing at the same time, when we two stayed up until midnight talking and sharing our thoughts*

Writing the Poem

Students close their eyes and take a few moments to recall their memories. After their memory meditation, students write their poems. Encourage line breaks so that the poem looks like a poem and not like a story.

- Students title their poem *For Old Times.*
- Students begin their poem with "A toast to old times."
- Begin the second line with "when" and their memory.
  For example: *When we two stayed up until midnight talking and sharing our thoughts*
- Students continue writing each memory on its own line.

Editing and Publishing

- Students read and edit poems with partners.
- Students draw an illustration of their memories.
- Make a class book or a bulletin board display.

Poet for New Year's Eve
Robert Burns Biography
January 25, 1759 - July 21, 1796

Robert Burns was born in an ancient village on the west coast of Scotland. Although his parents were poor farmers, they believed it was important that their son received a good education. He entered school at the age of six. He learned English, French and Latin. His father taught him reading, writing, arithmetic, history and geography. From a young age, he loved to read. In his reading, he was introduced to famous poets who stirred his imagination.

His family was poor and Burns was forced to work as a farm laborer. Unlike his father, he was not tied to the land for his financial existence. He looked down different avenues to ensure a living. For a short time he worked as a flax-dresser. He prepared the flax plant for a spinner to make thread and cloth. At 27, he began profiting from his poetry. In 1791, at age 32, he was appointed as an exciseman (a tax collector) and finally was able to give up farming.

Burns was a rebel and didn't pay attention to his strict Calvinist religion or to the social order of the day. He had a wild reputation and courted many women in his short life. His first love, Nelly Kirkpatrick, encouraged him to write poetry. *Handsome Nell* was his first song. Burns fathered many children, both in and out of wedlock. He met his future wife, Jean Armour, when he was 26. A year later he became a father of twins. Jean Amour and Robert Burns had nine children and Burns fathered at least four other children by other women. There are over nine hundred decendents in his family tree.

As a poet, Burns wrote mostly in Scottish dialect. His poetry became famous throughout Scotland. His first volume sold out immediately. He traveled to Edinburgh on a borrowed pony to publish his second edition of poetry. Upon his arrival in Edinburgh, he was greeted with the respect and admiration from the literary community. A year later, his second volume of poetry was published. Burns was also a lyricist.

Robert Burns was a handsome, eloquent and charismatic man. He made an everlasting impression not only in Scotand but also internationally. He was famous for his poetry and lyrics written in his beloved Scottish dialect. Burns is considered to be one of the greatest lyric poets, with one of his most famous lyrics being *Auld Lang Syne*. He died at age 37 and was buried with full civil and military honors. Many of his songs and poems became even more famous after his death. Burns is known as the national poet of Scotland and he has influenced much of Scottish literature.

Good Old Times
By Robert Burns

English Verse

Should old acquaintance be forgot,
and never brought to mind?
Should old acquaintance be forgot,
and good old times?

[Chorus:]
For old times since, my dear,
for good old times,
we'll drink a cup of kindness yet,
for good old times.

And surely you'll have your pint cup!
and surely I'll have mine!
And we'll drink a cup o' kindness yet,
for good old times.

(Chorus)
We two have run about the slopes,
and picked the daisies fine;
But we've wandered many a weary foot,
since good old times.

(Chorus)
We two have paddled in the stream,
from morning sun till dine;
But seas between us broad have roared
since good old times.

(Chorus)
And there's a hand my trusty friend!
And give us a hand o' thine!
And we'll take a right good-will draught,
for good old times.

Auld Lang Syne
by Robert Burns

Original Scots Verse

Should auld acquaintance be forgot,
and never brought to mind?
Should auld acquaintance be forgot,
and auld lang syne ?

[Chorus:]
For auld lang syne, my jo,
for auld lang syne,
we'll tak a cup o' kindness yet,
for auld lang syne.

And surely ye'll be your pint-stowp!
and surely I'll be mine!
And we'll tak a cup o' kindness yet,
for auld lang syne.

(Chorus)
We twa hae run about the braes,
and pu'd the gowans fine;
But we've wander'd mony a weary fit,
sin auld lang syne.

(Chorus)
We twa hae paidl'd i' the burn,
frae morning sun till dine;
But seas between us braid hae roar'd
sin auld lang syne.

(Chorus)
And there's a hand, my trsty fiere!
and gie's a hand o' thine!
And we'll tak a right gude-willy waught,
for auld lang syne.

Technology Lesson for National Write a Friend Month: Stationery Design

We text, we tweet, we chat, we Facebook and we email. In this digital age it is easy to forget the joy and pleasure of receiving a handwritten letter via snail mail. It is no surprise that December is "Write a Letter to a Friend Month." During the holiday season many families compose special letters for friends and family near and far. December 7th is designated as National Letter Writing Day. To join in the National Letter Writing Day celebration, students use technology to design their own personal stationery to use for their handwritten letters.

MATERIALS

- Technical devices with Internet and printer connections
- Printer (color preferred)
- Desktop publishing or paint/draw software
- Blank white or colored computer paper (stationery quality preferred)
- Whiteboard or chart paper with markers

PLAN

- Begin a class discussion by asking students to talk about letters they have written and received in snail mail.
- Discuss the categories of people to whom they would like to send a special letter.
- List the possibilities on the board (for example: parents, cousins, favorite past teachers, long-distance friends, etc.).

DO

- Students begin by deciding who will receive their handwritten letter.
- They open a blank page in their word processing or paint/draw program.
- Explain that in several word processing programs, when pictures are placed in a document they are inline pictures. Inline pictures move with the text. In order to use several graphics on one page, it is necessary to format imported pictures to have them float on the page using the wrap text menu on their word processor. They need to select the picture and use the menu to change the word wrap from being in line with text to wrap square or tight.
- Have students follow the directions below to create their own decorated stationery:
    - Use an Internet search engine to find clipart, graphics and borders.
    - Drag or copy and paste several graphics of their choice onto the page.
    - Remember to use the wrap text feature and make pictures wrap tight or wrap square to make them easy to manipulate.
    - Size, move and place graphics around the page until happy with the design.
    - Choose a paper on which to print the newly created stationery and print.
    - Students handwrite their letter on the stationery using a friendly letter format, which includes a heading, greeting, body, closing, and signature.
    - Students mail or hand-deliver their letter to the recipient.

National Write a Friend Month
Science Extension: Invisible Ink

Student scientists work in pairs to write invisible ink messages to their classmates. By dipping writing instruments in various acids or bases, students create a secret message. By uncovering the message with a pH indicator (red cabbage juice), students determine which words were written with an acid and which words were written with a base. A pH indicator is a special compound that becomes a different color on a pH scale when coming into contact with acids or bases.

MATERIALS

Invisible Ink Handout
Ammonia (base/alkaline), baking soda (base/alkaline), lemon juice (acid), vinegar (acid), red cabbage juice that you will make (pH indicator)
Glass containers
Large index cards
Measuring cups
Paper cups
Writing Instruments: paintbrushes, toothpicks or Q-tip
Universal pH color indicator chart (available on the Internet)

1. Discuss student knowledge of acids and bases. Perhaps they mixed baking soda (a base or alkaline) and vinegar (an acid) and watched as the mixture created erupting volcanoes. Some students may have used the reaction to power a toy boat, launch a rocket or blow up a balloon.
2. Display a universal pH color chart on the board or on a chart. These can be purchased, downloaded, or printed from the Internet. Discuss how the color indicators show the degree to which a substance is acidic, neutral or alkaline.
3. Prepare the red cabbage juice with student volunteers as follows:
   a. Chop up half a head of red cabbage into the smallest possible pieces and place in a glass container.
   b. Add enough boiling water to cover the cabbage.
   c. Let the cabbage sit for about twenty minutes or until the water is red.
   d. Strain the cabbage water through a coffee filter into a fresh container.
4. Distribute the Invisible Ink Handout.
5. Divide the class into pairs and distribute index cards, paint brushes or tooth picks, measuring cups and paper cups. Follow the directions on the worksheet for use of the other ingredients in the materials list.
7. Have students write their friendly messages and let the papers dry.
8. Have students exchange finished messages and follow the directions on the handout to decode each other's messages.

Invisible Ink Handout

1. Create a four-word friendly message with your partner.
2. Add about ¼ cup of water to a cup containing ¼ cup baking soda.
3. Add ¼ cup of water to a another cup containing ¼ red cabbage juice.
4. Dip the brush, toothpick or Q-tip (writing instrument) into the baking soda mixture and write the first word of your message.
5. Dip a fresh writing instrument into the cup containing vinegar and write the second word of your message.
6. Dip a fresh writing instrument into the cup containing lemon juice and write the third word of your message.
7. Dip a fresh writing instrument into the cup containing ammonia and write the fourth word of your message.
8. Let the paper dry. Possibly wave it in the air to dry it faster.
9. Exchange the finished messages with another pair of students.
10. Using a clean Q-tip or brush, rub cabbage juice all over the card to reveal the message.
11. The red cabbage water works as a pH color indicator to measure the strength of an acid or base. It ranges from the strongest acid (red) to the strongest base (yellow).
12. Place an X in the chart below to show the color changes as each word is uncovered with the red cabbage pH indicator.

Red Cabbage Color Changes

	0	2	4	6	8	10	12	14
	red	**light pink**	**dark pink**	**purple**	**blue**	**aqua**	**green**	**yellow**
baking soda								
vinegar								
lemon juice								
ammonia								

Poetry Lesson for National Write a Friend Month: O! why was I born with a different face?

In his letter poem to Thomas Butts *O! why was I born with a different face?* William Blake expresses honestly and poetically that he is feeling like an outsider when he writes "why was I not born like the rest of my race?" He also feels he can't do anything right "when I speak, I offend;/then I'm silent & passive & lose every friend." He conveys his distrust of himself as an artist "my verse I dishonour, my pictures despise." His letter reads like a poem because of its rhymes, line breaks and powerful intense poetic descriptions.

MATERIALS

- William Blake Biography and his poem *Oh! why was I born with a different face*
- Desktop publishing software
- Colored paper, pencils, crayons and other art supplies
- Envelopes (optional)

PLAN

- Read and discuss William Blake Biography and poem.
- Encourage responses to the following questions:
  - What makes Blake's letter to his friend sound like a poem rather than a letter?
  - What does he mean when he writes "why was I not born like the rest of my race?"
  - What does he write that makes us know that he is not feeling good about himself?
  - When does he feel that people envy him?
  - When does he feel they despise him?

DO

Getting Ready to Write

Discuss the following questions with students:

- Why would you want to share your feelings about yourself?
- If you shared your feelings about yourself with a friend in a letter, how do you think it would make you feel?
- If you were to share something about yourself that you do not like what would it be? For example: *curly hair or straight hair*
- What details would you write about this part of yourself that you do not like? For example: *my friends laugh at me, in the morning it's straight,* and *then it curls itself tight*

Writing the Poem

Students follow the steps below to write their poems. Suggest they write at least four lines.

- Title poems "To [the receipient of their letter]."
- Begin the first line of your poem with "Why was I born with [an aspect about yourself you do not like]?"
- Continue the poem describing what you don't like about this part of yourself.
- Each description should be on its own line.
- If you want to rhyme, feel free to do so.
- Use descriptive language.

Editing and Publishing

- Students handwrite or print their letter poems on construction paper or other writing paper.
- Decorate the paper using colored pencils or crayons.
- Students could fold and enclose their poems in decorated envelopes and mail them to their friends.

Why was I born with so many freckles?
Jack
4th grade

Poet for National Write a Friend Month
William Blake Biography
November 28, 1757 - August 12, 1827

William Blake was born in England. His parents were not wealthy but always supported his genius. When he was only four years old, he began to have visions. In one, he saw a tree filled with angels who sang and waved their wings in the branches. These visions were to become the subjects of his drawings and poetry throughout his life.

William's love of drawing and writing began at a very young age. Although he never attended school, he learned to read from his mother. When he was ten, his father, recognizing his artistic talent, sent him to drawing school. There he learned to develop his skills by copying prints in drawing books. His teacher at the school sent him to Westminster Abbey, a famous church in London. At the Abbey, he spent his time sketching the statues. These statues were a major influence on his drawings. At about age 14, he started writing poetry and combining his writing with his drawing.

As he walked along the streets of London, he saw children being mistreated and working very long hours in city factories. In his visions, he saw a different world. He saw angels dancing around the sun that shined over London and children laughing on clouds. He wrote about the innocence of children and much of his artistic energy was used to bring about a change in the way people behaved towards them.

His life of writing and working on engravings was interrupted for a brief time when one evening a drunken soldier came into Blake's garden. A fight started and Blake overcome with anger said some negative things about the king and his soldiers. The soldier and one of his friends communicated and exaggerated what Blake had said and he was tried for high treason. At trial, he was acquitted when his attorney and many of his neighbors attested to Blake's fine character. The trial must have been a difficult experience for Blake and he expressed his feelings in a letter poem to his friend *O! why was I born with a different face*? He truly was born with a different way of seeing his world.

[To Thomas Butts]: O! why was I born with a different face?
by William Blake

"Oh! why was I born with a different face?
Why was I not born like the rest of my race?
When I look, each one starts! when I speak, I offend;
Then I'm silent and passive and lose every friend.

Then my verse I dishonour, my pictures despise,
My person degrade & my temper chastise;
And the pen is my terror, the pencil my shame;
All my talents I bury, and dead is my fame.

I am either too low or too highly prized;
When elate I'm envy'd, when meek I'm despis'd"

Art Lesson for National Write a Friend Month: Crayon Resist

Artists use resist wax techniques where the wax crayon repels paint and paint adheres to the surrounding paper. Resist techniques are common in many textile patterns and also can be found in both tie dye and batik works of art. To celebrate National Write a Friend Month, students create works of art writing a special message to a friend using a crayon resist technique.

MATERIALS

Pencils
Paper
Light color crayons
Watercolors, preferably vivid colors
Water
Paper cups
Paint brushes

LESSON

Students do the following:

1. Brainstorm answers to the question, what is a friend?
   For example:
   A friend is someone who likes you.
   A friend is someone you can laugh with.
   A friend is someone you share your candy with.
   A friend is someone you can count on.
2. Students write their statement lightly in pencil on a piece of paper. Make it large enough to fill the sheet.
3. Trace over the writing with a light-colored crayon. Press hard.
4. Draw additional designs.
5. Paint over the message and designs with one or more vivid water colors.
6. Let the paintings dry.
7. Create a clothesline display and hang the finished pictures with clothespins.
8. Drape yarn on a bulletin board display and hang the finished messages with clothespins.

Engineering Lesson for Winter: How to Make a Soap (Ice) Carving

Children in colder climates enjoy carving winter ice sculptures. In this lesson, students in every climate will experience the fun of making soap carvings. Their sculptures won't melt and will make great holiday gifts.

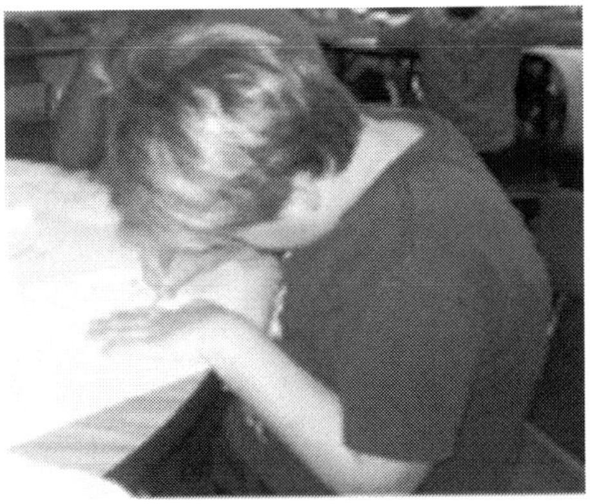

Jack
4th Grade

MATERIALS (for each group)

- Newspaper to cover tables
- Wrapped bar of soap (Ivory bars are recommended)
- Plastic or dull knives
- 3" x 4" rectangles of heavy paper
- Pencils with erasers
- Water and cotton swabs
- Examples of soap designs

PLAN

- Carving soap is a very messy but fun activity. You may want to limit this activity to one area in the room that is completely covered – floors, tables, etc.
- Students will be learning basic sculpting techniques in order to carve a soap sculpture. Whether they start with large blocks of ice or soap, the technique is the same. They remove the part of the soap that is not part of their design.
- Place 3" x 4" paper rectangles, soap design examples, pencils, plastic or dull knives, water, cotton swabs and wrapped bars of soap on tables. Also place toothpicks, skewers or other pointed objects to add details to the carvings.

DO

- Divide the class into small groups.
- Students decide on a design to carve. They can refer to the design examples on the table.
- Students draw their design on the heavy paper to create a template. Their design needs to fit on the bar of soap.
- They cut out the template and place it on the bar of soap and trace around the outline of the template with a pencil.
- Students scrape away small portions of the soap outside of the design with the knives. To avoid having the soap break off by itself into chunks, remind students to carefully scrape away small portions at a time.
- When the outside carving is finished, students add details to complete their design.
- After their carving is finished they rub it with their fingers or a wet cotton swab to make it smooth. Just a very small amount of water is needed.
- Dry the finished sculptures for a day to make sure the carvings harden.
- Students can display their sculptures, wrap them as presents or even use them as soap.

Technology Extension for Winter: Festive December

The winter months are filled with holidays and celebrations. In this lesson students will focus on festive December as they create a slide show featuring Christmas, Hanukah and Kwanzaa. They also can substitute one of their favorite December celebrations.

MATERIALS

- Internet access
- Multimedia presentation software (PowerPoint, HyperStudio, Keynote or Google Docs)
- Drawing software (Kid Pix, Tux Paint, Sketchpad)
- Photo editors such as Photoshop Elements, PIXLR (a free on-line photo editor)
- Storyboard planning worksheets, two copies per group
- Pencils and other drawing tools

PLAN

During a class discussion, students talk about celebrating December holidays.

- Tell them they are going to work in groups to plan and produce a slide show or a video showcasing celebrations that occur at Christmas, Hanukah and Kwanzaa.
- Create a class list of general and specific topics to include in the slide shows.
- Use the lists below to get started:
  - General Topics:
    - Holiday cards
    - Gift ideas
    - Recipes
    - Videos
    - Photos
    - Games
    - Holiday celebrations
    - Crafts
    - Family traditions
    - Word search and crossword puzzles
  - Specific Topics:
    - Christmas tree
    - Ornament
    - Dreidel
    - Kwanzaa Principles

DO

Student groups design and produce a multimedia presentation celebrating December Holidays by following the steps below:

- Use the December Holidays Planning Sheets to design the production and determine the content.
- Slide shows must consist of at least two frames per holiday and last no longer than three minutes.
- Search the Internet for information, pictures, videos, recordings and so on.
- Create a new document in the software program you will be using.
- Select layout, color scheme and text styles.
- Add text boxes along with researched multimedia elements.
- Select transitions.
- Play, review, revise and fine-tune the production.
- For extra pizzazz, import your multimedia presentation into movie-making software like iMovie or WeVideo. Use the program's features to change the look of your video and add a variety of transitions, fast/slow motion and/or green screen effects.

Festive December Planning Sheets

Use the topics below and some of your own to plan each slide.

holiday cards • gift ideas • recipes • videos • photos
games • holiday celebrations • crafts • family traditions
word search and crossword puzzles

Chistmas 1

Christmas 2

Hanukkah 1

Hanukkah 2

Use the topics below and some of your own to plan each slide.

holiday cards • gift ideas • recipes • videos • photos
games • holiday celebrations • crafts • family traditions
word search and crossword puzzles

Kwanzaa 1

Kwanzaa 2

Other December holiday

Other December holiday

Poetry Lesson for Winter: Winter Haikus

In Basho's winter haikus, he captures the stillness, cold and beauty of this season in diverse images: clouds that promise snow; the wind's sound; chrysanthemums and more. Through observation that is close to meditation, he brilliantly takes a moment and makes it last forever.

MATERIALS

- Matsuo Basho Biography and a selection of winter haikus
- Pencil, paper, word processing and/or desktop publishing software
- Chart or smart board

PLAN

Read and discuss Matsuo Basho's biography and the selection of winter haikus.

- Review the structure of the haiku that typically has three lines with five syllables in the first, seven syllables in the second and five in the third.
- Explain that Basho's poetry often loses the 5-7-5 pattern of haiku during the translation from Japanese to English.
- Tell students that each haiku is a scene about a moment in nature. Ask which is their favorite scene and why.
- Discuss the words Basho uses to capture the season and feeling of winter.

DO

Getting Ready to Write

Discuss with students the following questions:

  - What nouns, verbs, adjectives and adverbs does winter bring to mind?
  - What colors do you see and sounds do you hear when you think about winter?
- Chart responses.
- Have students refer to the words listed in writing a whole class haiku.
- Guide them through the process through editing and revising while creating a poem that has the haiku structure and conveys the feeling of winter.

Writing the Poem

- Students write their own winter poems using the haiku structure.
- Remind them to focus on the smallest details of a larger scene.

Editing and Publishing

- Students first read to themselves to check the 5-7-5 syllable structure.
- The poems by students are perfectly suited for a class anthology.
- Create and distribute the anthologies to the students and have a class read-around.

Poet for Winter
Matsuo Basho Biography
1644 - 1694

Matsuo Basho was born in Ueno, a small city in Japan. Japan had a society that consisted of classes. Basho was a Samurai. Unlike those in lower classes, Samurais were allowed to own their own land and receive an education. Basho was educated and learned Japanese and Chinese classics. When he was twelve, he began writing haiku, a form of Japanese poetry. At age 22, he had haikus published in anthologies and he began to teach haiku. His haikus were written in a plain language and about ordinary subjects. He thought that poetry should be written about experiences with nature because nature held the highest meaning in life. In his haikus, nature and the changes that occur in nature were important. Through nature, he expressed the emotions he felt. In his haikus, the seasons would often appear in either the first or third line of his three-line poems.

Often, in his travels, after he would reach the top of a hill, or when he would pause to take a rest, he would stop and look around. Basho saw beautiful energy flow around him – the golden sun bathing a valley or blooming trees by the path. He would also find the same beauty in much smaller things – tiny purse weed flowers under a bush or honeybees busy collecting nectar from flowers. This intense feeling of total awareness that often lasts just for a short moment Basho made permanent by describing it in his poems. By the time he was 34, Basho was considered a great poet and had several men studying with him.

Eventually Basho retired from the literary world. He shaved his head, became a Zen monk and moved to a small and extremely quiet area of Edo. He studied Chinese poetry and meditated. A fire destroyed much of Edo, and Basho's house burned to the ground. After the fire, Basho became disinterested in earthly possessions and began travelling. After three years of travel he returned to Edo. Basho no longer wanted to be involved with the literary world and thought of giving up the writing and teaching of poetry. Because of his love and dedication to both he continued writing and teaching until he died. He was dedicated to improving haiku and was responsible for making it one of the greatest forms of poetry in the literary world.

Winter Haikus
by Matsuo Basho

Even that old horse
is something to see
this snow-covered morning

...

Hello! Light the fire!
I'll bring inside
a lovely bright ball of snow

...

Crossing half the sky,
on my way to the capital,
big clouds promise snow

...

Winter garden,
the moon thinned to a thread,
insects singing.

...

Winter seclusion –
sitting propped against
The same worn post

...

Winter solitude--
In a world of one color
the sound of wind.

...

When the winter chrysanthemums go,
there's nothing to write about
but radishes.

...

First snow
falling
on the half-finished bridge.

...

The winter leeks
Have been washed white –
How cold it is!

Dance Lesson: Winter Interpretive Dance

In this lesson, students combine the winter sounds in Maurice Ravel's String Quartet in F Major with interpretative dance movements to express the emotions about winter the music evokes. Winter of all the seasons brings a sense of quiet with its soft winds and snow that muffles sounds. In Maurice Ravel's String Quartet, winter can be felt with the soft strings that call to mind an old frozen forest. You can almost hear the groaning of tree branches and the thawing of ice.

Interpretive dance, a form of modern dance, in which the dancer's movements depict emotions or tells a story, has its roots in many cultures. Isadora Duncan made interpretive dance popular in the early 1900s. She is known as the "mother of modern dance." From the age of six, she showed her genius while teaching movement to other children. She would go on to become famous in Europe and the United States.

MATERIALS

An audio recording of Maurice Ravel's String Quartet in F Major (from a CD, iTunes, etc.)
Device for playback

LESSON

1. Share with the class a short video about Isadora Duncan. https://www.youtube.com/watch?v=mKtQWU2ifOs
2. Play Ravel's String Quartet and have students listen for sounds that remind them of winter.
3. Discuss emotions the music evokes.
4. Students take a few quiet moments and allow themselves to drift into these emotions.
5. Encourage them to let go as if they are alone with these feelings.
6. Students begin to move allowing the music to guide them using their whole body.
7. Next students try isolating arms, legs, feet, and head.
8. Have student volunteers demonstrate some of their movements.
9. Divide the class into groups of five and have each group create an interpretive dance to Ravel's music.
10. After sufficient practice, each group performs their dance.

Mathematics Lesson for December Holidays: Shopping for Holiday Parties

In this activity, students work with a partner to go shopping on the Internet to purchase party items for a holiday party of twenty people. Their spending limit will be $200. They will be responsible for purchasing all the items they need for their party.

MATERIALS

- Internet access
- Paper and pencils
- Whiteboard or chart paper

PLAN

- During a class discussion, students talk about holiday parties.
- Tell them they are going to work with a partner to plan a party.
- This party will need to include items from the following categories: party essentials, decorations, accessories and food and beverages.
- As they name items, list them on a board or chart under the suggested categories.

DO

Working in pairs, students decide on a holiday party theme and do the following:

- Using pencil and paper, students make a list of items they wish to purchase from the following categories:
    1. Party essentials (invitations, plates, napkins, cutlery, drinking cups, etc.)
    2. Decorations
    3. Accessories (party favors, games, etc.)
    4. Food and beverages
- Students first purchase all essential items on their list.
- Using the search engine of their choice, students explore a few party and grocery sites before selecting the ones they will use.
- To create a balance sheet, students divide a paper into thirds. They write the following titles, one on top of each column: Item, Price, Balance.
- Students begin by writing $200.00 on the first line in the balance column.
- Next, students write the name of the first item they wish to purchase and its price on the second line under the appropriate columns.
- Students subtract the cost of the item in dollars and cents from the $200 and write the new balance.
- Students continue to shop until they reach or are close to a zero balance.
- When students are finished they can check their work in one of two ways:
    - Exchange papers and check each other's calculations.
    - Open a spreadsheet, create three columns, write the headings for each column and enter the data from their worksheet to check their bookkeeping.

Engineering Extension for December Holidays: Gumdrop Bridge Challenge

In this STEM challenge student engineers work in small groups to construct a bridge across an abyss between two even stacks of books using toothpicks and gumdrops. Each group will compete to build a bridge that supports a paper cup placed on top of the bridge. The bridge that can hold the most number of miniature candy canes or chocolate coins wins.
Each bridge is built to hold a cup of miniature candy canes or gold chocolate coins.

MATERIALS
Gumdrops (thirty for each group of four or five students)
Toothpicks
Small paper cups
Books
Miniature candy canes or chocolate gold coins
Engineering Journal Gumdrop Bridge Challenge Handout

1. Discuss previous student experiences with building structures. What have they learned? Do they have any advice to share?
2. Talk about how the strengths of shapes (such as triangles, squares, pentagons) influences the structure's ability to stand and hold weight.
3. Tell class they will work in groups. Each group will use a maximum of 30 gumdrops and 30 toothpicks to build bridges strong enough to hold a cup filled with miniature candy canes or chocolate gold coins. The group whose cup holds the greatest amount of candy will win the challenge.
4. Divide the class into groups of four or five students. Distribute 30 gumdrops, 30 toothpicks and the Engineering Journal Gumdrop Bridge Challenge Handout.
5. Students use the journal handout during the planning, building and evaluation stages of the challenge.
6. Each group builds two equal stacks of books approximately a foot high.
7. Challenge students to design and create a gumdrop and toothpick bridge between the two stacks that will hold the greatest number of candy canes or chocolate gold coins in a cup placed on top of the bridge. The bridge span must be at least six inches.
8. Students plan, build and test their designs.
9. After building and testing, students evaluate the results and make modifications to improve their structure.
10. Each group presents their final bridge structure. Students add the candy to the cup, one piece at a time, to see how many the bridge cup will hold before the bridge collapses. A winning group is determined.
11. Students reflect on the challenge and enter their thoughts into the journal.

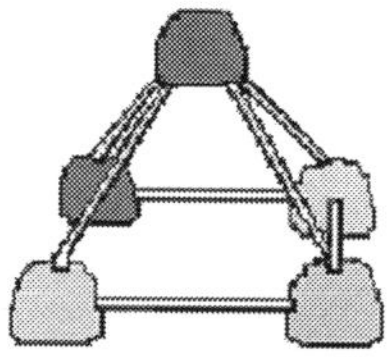

Engineering Journal
Gumdrop Bridge Challenge

State the Problem

Draw a Diagram

Describe the Solution

Describe Modifications

Reflections

Poetry Lesson for December Holidays: little tree

What better way to think about the December holidays than with the poem *little tree* by e. e. Cummings? In this poem, Cummings speaks to a symbol of Christmas, a tree. Children will think about the different winter holidays through the symbols that represent each.

MATERIALS

- e. e. Cummings Biography and his poem *little tree.*
- Pencil, paper, word processing and/or desktop publishing software
- Chart or smart board

PLAN

Read and discuss the biography of e. e. Cummings and his poem *little tree.*

- Cummings did not use punctuation or capitalization except for the words "Christmas" and "Noel." In this poem, Cummings only capitalized words referring to God including Noel, a French word meaning Christ's birthday.
- Discuss personification. Where does Cummings use personification?
- Call attention to his use of arms rather than branches and fingers rather than twigs.

DO

Getting Ready to Write

- During a brainstorming session, use the following discussion points and questions. As the class gives their responses, list them on the board or on a chart.
  - The "little tree" is a symbol for one of the December holidays, Christmas. What other holidays are in December?
  - What symbols are there for each of these holidays?
- Write a sample poem with the class using a December holiday other than Christmas. Replace the title *little tree* with a symbol representing that holiday. Give the symbol human feelings and human form. Prompt the students to include the symbol's past, present and future.

Writing the Poem

- Students write a poem to a symbol, as if they are speaking to it, using personification.
- Remind them that they refer to their symbol with "you" as the pronoun.
- Refer to the poem and the board examples for ideas. Their symbol can be used as the title.

Editing and Publishing

- Students read and edit poems with partners.
- Students write their poems in a poetry book or enter them in a word processing program and illustrate their poetic works.

Poet for December Holidays
e. e. cummings Biography
September 3, 1894 - October 14, 1962

Edward Estlin Cummings (known as e.e. cummings) was born in Cambridge, Massachusetts in 1894. His father was a minister. Cummings received a B.A. degree at Harvard in 1915 and a M.A. in 1916.

After Cummings graduated from Harvard, he went to France as a volunteer during World War I. In France, he was suspected of being an enemy and was put into a French detention center for three months. He eventually wrote a book about the people whom he met in this camp. He respected their ability to keep their spirits high in such a horrible environment.

After the war, Cummings lived in Paris and began painting and writing. It was there that he had his first book of poetry published. He was one of the most original of modern poets, dropping most punctuation and capitalization.

Many of his poems were about people who tried to ruin the natural world and about people who were opposed to freedom. He made friends with the poor and wrote poems honoring them. He admired above all else the freedom that children express. In his writing, he never lost that freedom. He writes with a childlike wonder and humor.

Cummings was a modern day Robin Hood who loved the poor. He was humorous, affectionate, and tough. Instead of carrying a bow and arrow to fight the everyday wrongs that he saw in society, he used words.

Poet for December Holidays
little tree
e. e. cummings

NOTE: *The entire poem is available online. Search for "little tree" by e. e. cummings or you can go to the following website and find the poem. It is ready to print, copy, and share with your class.*

http://www.poetryfoundation.org/poem/176724

The poem *little tree* is perfect for children because it is easily understood. Cummings uses personification in almost every line of the poem. He questions "little tree," by asking it "who found you in the green forest/and were you very sorry to come away?" To him, the "little tree" is sad and throughout the poem he comforts it by saying "i will kiss your cool bark/ and hug you safe and tight." Even its ornaments become alive and human as he writes that they have been sleeping in a box and "dreaming of being taken out and allowed to shine." The tree's branches are arms and its twigs are fingers as he tells the tree "to put up your little arms" and "every finger shall have its ring" so it can be dressed with decorations.

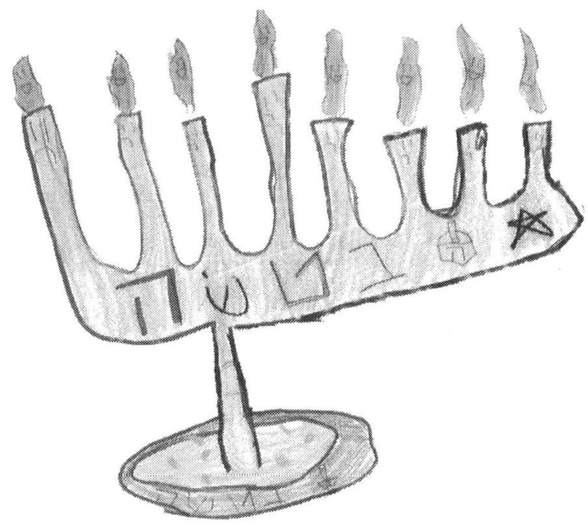

Matthew – 4th grade

Vasilisa – 4th grade

Poetry Lesson for December Holidays: Holidays

In his poem *Holidays,* Henry Wadsworth Longfellow writes "that the holiest of all holidays" are those that bring us tender memories. These memories are enhanced by descriptive similes. With similes, students write poems capturing the feelings of one particular winter holiday that brought them tender memories.

MATERIALS

- Henry Wadsworth Longfellow Biography and his poem *Holidays*
- Word processing or desktop publishing software or pencils, pens and paper

PLAN

- Read and discuss Henry Wadsworth Longfellow's biography and poem.
- Ask the following questions:
  - What does Longfellow express about holidays?
  - What similes are found in the poem?
  - What does the color white represent in the poem?

DO

Getting Ready to Write

Ask students the following questions. As they give their responses, encourage discussion. Before discussion, tell students that a simile compares one thing to another, using the word "as" or "like". Write answers on the board.

- What similes can be used to describe holiday memories that bring happiness to mind? For example: *peaceful as my grandmother singing a lullaby, gentle as my grandfather's kiss placed on my cheek, warm as the fire place on that night*

Writing the Poem

Students write poems using similes to describe memories of their winter holiday. Encourage line breaks so that the poem looks like a poem and not like a story.

- Students title their poems "Memories of My Winter Holiday."
- Suggest they begin their poems with the line: *Memories I will keep forever for they are*
- On the next line, continue the poem with a simile. For example: *peaceful as my grandmother singing a lullaby*
- Repeat each line using another simile.
- Students write at least four similes.

Editing and Publishing

- Students read and edit poems with partners.
- Students write their poems in a poetry book or compose their poems in a word processing program.
- Students illustrate their poems and give copies to people with whom they have shared their tender holiday.

Poet for December Holidays
Wadsworth Longfellow Biography
February 27, 1807 - March 24, 1882

Henry Wadsworth Longfellow was born in Portland, Maine. He became one of America's most famous poets. His father was a lawyer and it was thought that he would follow in his footsteps. However, Longfellow loved languages and poetry. At thirteen, he had his first poem published.

Longfellow studied at Boudin College where he showed a great talent for languages. In 1825 at the age of eighteen, Longfellow graduated fourth in his class. He was promised a position at Boudin if he would continue his education in Europe. He traveled through Europe for three years. These travels influenced his writing. After returning from Europe, he taught modern languages at Boudin and was also a university librarian. During this time, he was a translator and produced a great deal of creative writing and poetry.

Longfellow was offered a position at Harvard University as a professor of modern of languages. Before beginning his position, he again traveled to Europe to continue his study languages. After returning to the United States, Longfellow became a professor at Harvard where he taught English for twenty years. In 1854, after many years there, Longfellow resigned so that he could spend his time and energy on his poetry. He was able to support himself as a poet. He wrote powerful poems supporting the Abolitionist Movement, a movement to end slavery. His most famous poem, *Paul Revere's Ride,* is an American classic. The poem took poetic license and may not be historically correct.

Longfellow married twice. His first wife died at a young age. He fathered six children with his second wife. She died in a tragic house fire. These losses left him distraught. In spite of his losses, Longfellow always tried to place himself in positive situations. He loved sunshine, the sky, the sounds of nature and the differences that each season presented. He wrote about all of the wonders he experienced. His faith and optimism about life gave him the energy to write great poetry. He said: "We have but one life here on earth, and we must make that beautiful."

In later years, Longfellow received honorary degrees at Oxford and Cambridge. Queen Victoria invited him to Windsor Castle. Longfellow was chosen a member of the Russian Academy of Sciences and of the Spanish Academy. He is the only American to be honored with a bust placed in the Poet's Corner of Westminster Abbey.

Holidays

by Henry Wadsworth Longfellow

The holiest of all holidays are those
    Kept by ourselves in silence and apart;
    The secret anniversaries of the heart,
    When the full river of feeling overflows;--
The happy days unclouded to their close;
    The sudden joys that out of darkness start
    As flames from ashes; swift desires that dart
    Like swallows singing down each wind that blows!
White as the gleam of a receding sail,
    White as a cloud that floats and fades in air,
    White as the whitest lily on a stream,
These tender memories are;- a fairy tale
    Of some enchanted land we know not where,
    But lovely as a landscape in a dream.

January Monthly Holidays

Children's Vision and Learning Month • Foot Health Month • Harvest Month • International Air Travel Month • National Back to School Month • National Catfish Month • National Golf Month • National Inventor's Month • National Parks Month • National Water Quality Month • Peace Month

January Weekly Holidays

First Week of January
Braille Literacy Week • National Lose Weight-Feel Great Week • New Year's Resolution Week

Second Week of January
Cuckoo Dancing Week • Elvis Presley Birthday Celebration Week • Healthy Weight Week • National Pizza Week • Universal Letter Writing Week

Third Week of January
Celebrity Read-a-Book Week • Fresh Squeezed Juice Week • Hunt for Happiness Week • International Printing Week • National Clean Out Your In-Box Week • National Thrift Week • No Name Calling Week

Last Week of January
Catholic Schools Week • Junior Achievement Week • National Handwriting Analysis Week • National School Choice Week

January Moveable Holidays

National Weigh-In Day .... first Monday

National Clean-Off-Your-Desk-Day .... second Monday

Martin Luther King Day of Service .... third Monday

Bubble Wrap® Appreciation Day .... last Monday

Fun-at-Work-Day .... last Friday

January Days for STEM Makers and Poets

		Day	Make and Do
1		Ellis Island Day	Twelve million immigrants passed through the halls of Ellis Island from 1892 to 1954. The National Park Service offers distance learning, curriculum materials and more through the Ellis Island website at www.nps.gov/elis/index.htm. What countries did your ancestors come from? Create a map and a family tree.
2		National Science Fiction Day	Famous science fiction writer Isaac Asimov was born on this day in 1920 in Petrovichi, Russia. He wrote over 500 books. He is considered the father of robotics, a term he coined. Many of his science fiction writings have become reality. Imagine what the world will be like when you are 20 years old. Write a story or create a two-character science fiction play that includes new technologies that we currently only dream about. Will you be riding Hyperloop high-speed transports to travel from Los Angeles to New York in less than an hour? Will you fly to work in a drone? Illustrate your story or create a backdrop for your play.
3		National Drinking Straw Day	Today is National Drinking Straw Day. Back in 1956, Flav-R-Straws were introduced. Each straw included a chocolate or strawberry flavor. In honor of National Drinking Straw Day, in teams, build a straw structure. Using 50 straws and 50 straight pins, students have 15 minutes to build the tallest, freestanding structure that they can.
4		Trivia Day	Create a science trivia board game to play with your friends. Choose an area of science that interests you. If you want to make an interactive science trivia game, check out Kahoot. You can find it at getkahoot.com.

5		National Bird Day	Bird lovers celebrate annually with a variety of activities. "Birding" is a hobby in which individuals enjoy bird study, observing local species and maintaining lists of birds they have seen in their lifetime. Backyard birding is popular. On National Bird Day, design and build a birdhouse. What safety concerns must you consider? First build a scale model to test and tweak your design.
6		National Bean Day	Some believe that National Bean Day commemorates the death of geneticist Gregor Mendel in 1884 who famously used beans and pea plants to demonstrate his theories on inheritance. It's a great day to play Bean Nim. Nim is a math game where both payers have exactly the same information and chance plays no part. Start with a pile of dried beans. Alternate turns by taking up to three beans and you may not pass. The loser takes the last bean. What was your winning strategy? Try replaying the game, but this time the winner is the one who takes the last bean.
7		International Programmer's Day	Celebrate by exploring Scratch, a programming language and online community developed by Mitchel Resnick at the MIT Media Lab and launched in 2006. You can find Scratch at http://scratch.mit.edu. Scratch is a free programming platform that lets you create interactive stories, games and animations. Scratch users embrace their slogan: "Imagine, Program, Share." What will you program today? Begin by checking out the tutorial.
8		Bubble Bath Day	For over 50 years, Mr. Bubble continues to be the best-selling bubble bath in the USA. Become a product engineer and make your own customized bubble bath. Start with ½ cup of shampoo, dish soap, hand soap or Castile soap. Add one tablespoon of honey as a moisturizer or choose from olive, almond or jojoba oil. Add an egg white to help keep your bubbles big and strong. Lastly, add five drops of the essential oil of your choice. Select lavender, lemon or sandalwood. Shake it up in a plastic container. What will you name your creation? Design a label for your bubble bath.

9		National Static Electricity Day	Try some simple experiments with static electricity. For example, use a balloon and some tissue paper to demonstrate static electricity. What happens when you use a comb that you have run through your hair ten times?
10		National Cut Your Energy Costs Day	The world's supply of energy is limited and dependent upon many nonrenewable energy resources. Energy is consumed when we plug in an appliance or start up a car. The depletion of fossil fuels is a serious global issue. Americans use six times the energy as the average person in other countries. The three most common uses are for comfort (heating and cooling); household activities (entertainment, lighting, cooking); and transportation. Research and determine three decisions you can make that will reduce your own energy consumption.
11		Amelia Earhart Day	As the first woman aviator, Amelia Earhart flew solo across the Atlantic Ocean. She was an aviation pioneer, author and educator. Earhart disappeared over the Pacific Ocean in 1937. The sixteenth woman to earn a pilot license, Amelia's life is still fascinating and studied. Discover ten facts and along with photos and video clips develop a multimedia presentation. The Library of Congress Smithsonian Institution website and the Amelia Earhart official website will get you started.
12		National Pharmacist Day	Today is a great day to consider a career in pharmacology. Pharmacists are a vital part of a healthcare team in your local hospital or community pharmacy. What does it take to become a pharmacist? Visit your neighborhood pharmacy and interview a pharmacist. Prepare five questions for the interview.
13		Skeptics Day	A skeptic is a person who questions or doubts accepted opinions. Do you believe that it is bad luck to walk under a ladder? Do you think there is a pot-of-gold at the end of a rainbow? Does chicken soup cure colds? Make a list of five things you are skeptical about and five things you are not. Research to find out if you have reason to be skeptical.

14		National Dress Up Your Pet Day	Even pets need a dress-up day. Snap a picture of your favorite pet (or find one one the Internet). Create an outfit out of paper, complete with accessories. Research dressed-up pets on the Internet for inspiration.
15		National Hat Day	Hats can keep our heads safe from the elements, show off our personal style; and perhaps identify our status or career choice. Design and make a hat that fits your personality. Decide what kind of hat you would like to make. Think about color, pattern, style and fabric. Sketch a design. Gather the materials you need, measure your head size and get going. Take a selfie in your finished hat.
16		Appreciate A Dragon Day	Dragons play an important role in mythology and folklore. "A dragon lives forever but not so girls and boys" is a lyrical line from the song "Puff, the Magic Dragon." The song lyrics were written by Leonard Lipton at age 19, inspired by the Ogden Nash poem "Custard the Dragon." Peter Yarrow wrote the music and Peter, Paul and Mary introduced the song Puff the Magic Dragon to the world in 1962. Listen to their song about Little Jackie Paper and his dragon named Puff. Imagine you had your own dragon. Write a poem or a story about your adventures. Draw a picture of your dragon.
17		Kid Inventors' Day	Water skis, popsicles and earmuffs were all invented by kids. Today is Kid Inventors' Day and also the birth anniversary of Benjamin Franklin. Franklin, an inventor and statesman, was one of our nation's greatest founding fathers. At age 12 he invented swim flippers. Check out the kidinventorsday.com website. Plan a Kid Inventors' Day for your class or your school. The website has many ideas to get you started.
18		Thesaurus Day	How do you engineer a snowman? It's winter and a great day to design and build a snowman in parts of the country. Word process directions to build a snowman using an adjective in each step. Share the directions with a friend. Together, use an on-line thesaurus to find substitutions for your adjectives. Print out your completed directions using a fancy font, borders and other illustrations.

19		National Popcorn Day	What's popping? Let's engineer a popcorn sculpture. Microwave one-quarter cup butter and a bag of mini-marshmallows until it liquefies and pour over 12 cups of pre-popped popcorn. Working quickly, sculpt your masterpiece. Before it hardens add other decorative items such as pretzels, Fruit Loops, raisins, hard candy, jellybeans and more.
20		Camcorder Day	This is a day for all videographers. Although the camcorder was introduced in 1983, it is rarely used today. Smart phones and other devices easily record video. Create a one-minute video about inventions that we no longer use today.
21		Granola Bar Day	Granola is great for breakfast or a snack and consists of a variety of ingredients including rolled oats, fruit, honey and nuts. When formed into granola bars, the results are similar to candy bars and depending upon ingredients, there is limited nutritional difference. Why not create a healthy bake or no-bake granola bar? What will your bar consist of? List the ingredients. Name your bar and design the wrapper.
22		National Answer Your Cat's Question Day	Cats use visual, vocal, olfactory and tactile modalities to communicate to other animals and to humans. If your cat could talk, what would he ask you? Just like your feline friend, you don't have to answer. Just sit and stare. Some people believe their cat can speak a number of recognizable words. For National Answer Your Cat's Question Day, write five questions that your cat might ask you if cats could talk. Write your answers. How do other animals communicate? Research to find several fun facts about animal communication.
23		National Handwriting Day	Today we celebrate the birthday of John Hancock, a founding father. He signed the Declaration of Independence with a signature bigger than anyone else. Today, practice your own personal signature. Try making just one letter stand out just like John. Another fun activity is to create a Hirschfeld-style drawing. Al Hirschfeld hid the name of his daughter, Nina, in each of his caricatures. View some of Hirschfeld's work and create a work of art, hiding your first name or signature.

24		National Peanut Butter Day	Today is National Peanut Butter Day. Invent the best peanut butter sandwich ever. Write the recipe and list the ingredients and quantity. Using a spreadsheet, calculate the cost of making your peanut butter sandwich for everyone in your class. You will need to determine the cost of your ingredients by checking out serving sizes and prices on the Internet.
25		Observe the Weather Day	It may be raining, snowing or sunny, but on Observe the Weather Day go outside and practice being a weather person. Note the temperature, wind and cloud coverage. Along with your observations, check out weather.com and write and record a weather report. If you aspire to be a television weather person, video your report.
26		Ground-breaking day of Disneyland in 1954.	Disneyland, everyone's favorite amusement park, is located in Anaheim, California. Walt Disney conceived Disneyland as a combination of Tivoli Gardens in Copenhagen, Denmark and Greenfield Village in Dearborn, Michigan. Design your own amusement park. What sights will you include? Draw a map and design the rides and attractions. Why not build a diorama or an i [illegible] ark?
27		Bubble Wrap® Appreciation Day	Celebr [illegible] this day m [illegible] is nothin [illegible] poppi [illegible] p® Appre [illegible] s invent [illegible] garag [illegible] to make [illegible] g. Not su [illegible] rlene creati [illegible] ning mater [illegible] ad with c [illegible] s, and e [illegible] a Pop-A [illegible] l sculpture contests. You can even set up a game of Bubble Wrap Hopscotch. Cut out ten sheets of bubble wrap the size of a piece of letter-sized paper. Write the numbers one through ten on the smooth side. Lay out and get hopping.

28		Christa McAuliffe Day	Today we honor Christa McAuliffe who tragically died in the Space Shuttle Challenger. NASA's Educator Astronaut Project continues to excite students in math, science, and space exploration. What have we learned from space exploration? Create a slide show and record your voice to showcase your knowledge.
29		Puzzle Day	Be it crosswords, jumbles, jigsaws or sudoku, puzzles are lots of fun. Have a puzzle day party and set up competitions. Logic puzzles are fun to solve and to create. You can even plan online at www.logic-puzzles.org.
30		Escape Day	Give me a break; it's Escape Day! To where would you like to escape? Think of three great escapes and create your very own escape brochure for one of them. Your brochure could include a brief summary of your destination; activities to do when you get there; historic sites and landmarks; enticing photographs; the climate; and local food and customs.
31		Backwards Day	It's Backwards Day and it's a great day to do it all in reverse. *?day backward for do you will What.* Plan a Backwards Day for your class. What will you do? Make a list of ten backward activities. Will you wear your clothes inside out? Will you have breakfast for dinner? Document your day with photos, stories and poems and create a commemorative scrapbook highlighting your day. In reverse of course.

January Overview

Celebration of Life Month
Science Lesson: Celebrating Laughter Scientifically
Poetry Lesson: from Song of Myself by Walt Whitman
With this month's theme we reflect and appreciate each day of our life and recognize that life is precious. Students work in groups to explore laughter scientifically. Using Whitman's Song of Myself as a model, students write a catalog poem celebrating life.

Martin Luther King, Jr. Day
Technology Lesson:
Presenting Dr. Martin Luther King, Jr.
Poetry Lesson:
Hold Fast to Dreams by Langston Hughes
This day was established to remember and honor Dr. King and his work in the civil rights movement. Thematically, students use their technology skills to create a slide show highlighting his life. Using Langston Hughes' poem as a model, students write about the importance of dreams.

International Thank You Day
Engineering Lesson: Assembly Line Thank You Notes
Poetry Lesson: Thanksgiving by Ralph Waldo Emerson
We celebrate this day by taking the time to say thank you to the people in our lives and let them know they are appreciated. Student engineers work in a group assembly line to increase productivity as they create fancy thank you notes. In this poetry lesson, students reflect upon and write about the people and things in their lives for which to give thanks.

New Year's Day
Math Lesson: Calendar Challenge
Poetry Lesson: New Year by Ella Wheeler Wilcox
In the United States, we think of the New Year as a time to begin again with new hopes and dreams. Students use a New Year's calendar as they work in groups to create mathematical word problems. In the poetry lesson, students speak to the "New Year" telling what they will do to make it a good one.

Science Lesson for Celebration of Life Month: Celebrating Laughter Scientifically

An excellent way to celebrate life is to laugh more. Some of laughter's many physical and mental health benefits are boosting immunity, relaxing muscles, relieving stress, improving moods and adding joy to life. In addition, laughter celebrates life by strengthening relationships, promoting group bonding and enhancing teamwork. In this lesson, students will work in groups to devise experiments to test laughter scientifically by creating situations that produce laughter culminating in a classroom comedy theatre.

MATERIALS

- Chart paper or smart board
- Internet access
- Paper, pencils
- Exploring Laughter Handout and Science Experiment Handout
- Camera (optional)

PLAN

- Distribute and discuss the various claims about laughter on the Exploring Laughter Handout.
- Demonstrate one way in which the claim that laughter is contagious can be explored scientifically using the scientific method.
- Construct a group **hypothesis** about what students think will happen if the class sits in a circle facing each other and everyone begins to laugh (forced laughter is fine).
- Write the hypothesis on a chart or board.
- Discuss the **procedure** they will follow as they perform the experiment. Write the following procedure on the chart or board.
    1. Sit in circle.
    2. Keep body still (no cat-falls etc.).
    3. Keep natural facial expressions (no silly faces).
    4. No talking or noise-making.
- Begin to laugh.
- After two or three minutes, stop the laughter.
- Write student **observations** on the board or chart.
- Write the **results** on the board or chart.
- Write a **conclusion.** Was the hypothesis correct?
- Discuss ways to further test whether laughter is contagious. For example: Would the results be different if they turned their backs to each other while in the circle and laughed? Would the sound of laughter alone be contagious?

DO

- Read and discuss the Exploring Laughter Handout.
- Review the scientific method by going over the steps with the Science Experiment Handout.
- Divide the class into four to six groups and have each group choose a topic for their experiment.
- As they perform each step in the experiment, have students record the results.
- If possible, encourage students to take photos during the process.
- Have each group design a presentation of their experiment to share with the class.

3rd grade girls

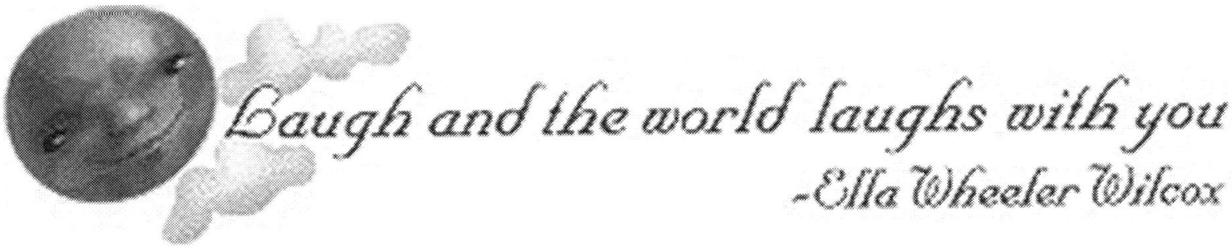

Exploring Laughter Handout

Below is a list of common beliefs about laughter. Pick a belief from the list or add one and create a group project to test and record the results of that belief.

Laughter is a form of exercise.

Laughter is catching (hearing it, seeing it, both).

Laughter is the best medicine.

A person who makes others laugh has power over the emotional climate of the group.

Boys tell jokes better than girls.

Most class clowns are boys.

Girls laugh at jokes more often than boys.

Girls giggle more and longer than boys.

The best ways to make people laugh are:

- Joke telling
- Practical jokes
- Physical actions
- Funny facial expressions
- Slapstick comedy
- Silly noises

Words that have a hard "c" sound are funny, like cookie.

What beliefs would you add?

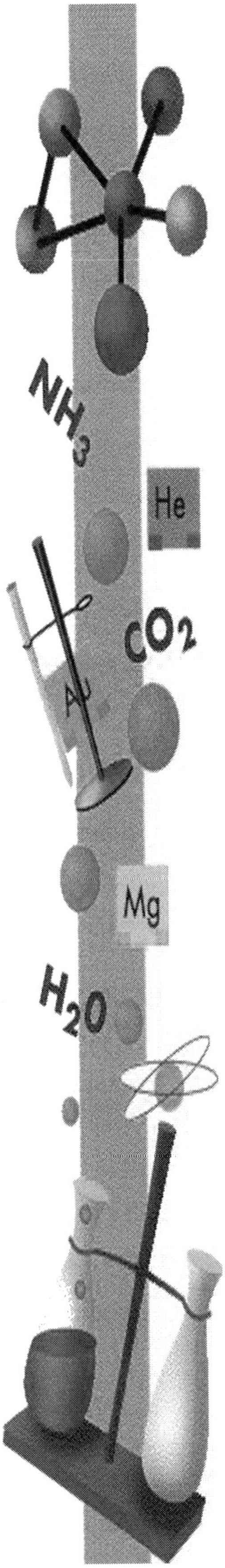

ScienceExperiment Handout

Inquiry: (Question to explore)

Observation: (What you notice)

Hypothesis: (Prediction)

Materials: (Supplies needed)

Procedure: (Steps)

Results: (What happened)

Conclusion: (Results)

Technology Extension for Celebration of Life Month: To Life

An ideal way to get off to a good start as the New Year begins is to plan Celebration of Life Month activities that help you to relax and enjoy yourself. January is a good time to start appreciating the lives that we lead, and the blessings that come to us every day. Celebration of Life Month allows us time to reflect on and appreciate each day of our life and to recognize that life is precious and should always be enjoyed and savored.

In this lesson, students will reflect on the little things that contribute to their enjoyment and zest for life. Thy use their reflections to create an individual slide for a group multimedia presentation. For example, they might think about the way their dog is always looking out the window waiting for them when they come home from school or how they are on a soccer team and look forward to their weekly games. Perhaps they have learned to play a musical instrument or look forward to watching movies with their family on Sunday evenings.

1. Divide the class into small brainstorming groups.
2. Have the group members share things in their lives that they appreciate.
3. After brainstorming, give each student time to create an individual list of at least five things that make life enjoyable.
4. Have individual group members plan the creation of a single slide to be included in the group presentation using software such as PowerPoint, Keynote, Google Slides or Prezi.
5. Have students select fonts, graphics, music, digital images or videos to symbolize each item on their list.
6. Suggest the use of personal digital pictures and videos to augment items found on the Internet.
7. Students work in their group to put their completed individual slides into a final group presentation as follows:
   a. Create a title slide.
   b. Decide on slide order and import each slide.
   c. Add transitions, animations, sounds and so on.
   d. Show off the group Celebration of Life Slide Show.

Poetry Lesson for Celebration of Life Month: Song of Myself

There couldn't be a more ideal poet to represent Celebration of Life Month than Walt Whitman. In his epic poem, *Song of Myself*, he celebrates himself by stating "the song of me rising from bed and meeting the sun." He includes in his celebration everything in creation that he experiences, starting with the smallest "spear of summer grass." The poem is Whitman's journey where he learns about himself through first-hand experiences and advises his readers that they must take their own journey to discover who they are, "You shall not look through my eyes either, nor take things from me, /You shall listen to all sides and filter them from your self." Whitman extols "The smoke of my own breath" to the entire universe and to all time. He is the universe – a part of all present and past as he makes his celebrated journey. Whitman uses a poetic technique known as catalog and he lists all people, animals and objects he meets on his journey. They become part of him just as he becomes part of them.

MATERIALS

- Walt Whitman Biography and his poem *Song of Myself*
- Word processing or desktop publishing software or pencils, pens and paper
- Board or chart

PLAN

- Read and discuss Walt Whitman's biography.
- Read and discuss *Song of Myself* using the following questions:
  - What does Whitman celebrate?
  - What does he mean when he states, "For every atom belonging to me, as good belongs to you?"
  - What kind of learning does he think is the most valuable?

DO

Getting Ready to Write

- During a brainstorming session, ask students to review the following questions and discussion points. As they give their responses, list them on the board or on a chart.
  - What things about yourself do you celebrate?
    For example: *your laughter, your smiling face, your great hugs*
  - What are the most memorable experiences that you celebrate?
    For example: *reading a book with your mother*
  - What are the most memorable things in nature that you celebrate?
- Have class expand each item on the list using metaphors, similes, descriptions and personification.

Writing the Poem

Students write a catalog poem. A catalog poem begins with a list. Have students write at least a ten-line poem as follows:

- Suggest students title their poem "Song of My Life."
- Begin the first line with the words "I celebrate life."
- Begin the second line with something about their body. For example: *my beating heart*
- Continue the poem by listing other aspects of themselves, their experiences, and things in nature, each on a separate line. For example:

  The freckles that sit on my nose
  reading a book with my grandmother
  the shade of the oak tree.
- Students may expand and enhance each item on their list.

Editing and Publishing

- Have students read and edit poems with partners.
- Students compose or publish their poems in a word processing program.
- Students illustrate their final masterpieces.
- Extend the lesson by putting together some of the best lines from each poem to create a class poem.

Poet Biography for Celebration of Life Month
Walt Whitman Biography
May 31, 1819 - March 26, 1892

Walt Whitman was born in Long Island, New York. His parents could not read or write very well. Walt lived part of his childhood on a farm on Long Island and part in the city of Brooklyn. He was very smart but seemed to be lazy and in a dream world.

He left school when he was eleven years old and worked at many different jobs. Although eleven seems very young to us now, it was not uncommon in the 1800s for a child to leave school at a young age.

After years of searching Whitman became a journalist. It was a perfect profession for him because he loved to write. After working for many newspapers, he was offered a job in New Orleans, Louisiana. In the 1800s, travelling from New York to Louisiana was a very long trip. On his travels to Louisiana he had the opportunity to see much of America. He traveled the open roads, down rough rivers and across the land.

As he traveled, Whitman saw much of this country and met many different people. He felt lucky for the kind of education he received through his travels. He believed the only way to understand something was to experience it first-hand. The cities and people he saw on his travels became subjects for much of his poetry.

Whitman's poetry sings with the freedom he felt as he travelled. He developed a form of poetry called free verse. Instead of restricting himself to accepted formulas for writing poetry, Whitman wrote as he spoke. His poetic lines were the natural flow and pauses of his own speech. His voice became a symbol of our country, where people have the freedom to express themselves, each in their own way.

Excerpt from Song of Myself
by Walt Whitman

I celebrate myself, and sing myself,
And what I assume you shall assume,
For every atom belonging to me, as good belongs to you.

. . .

I loafe and invite my soul;
I lean and loafe at my ease, observing a spear of summer grass.

. . .

The smoke of my own breath,
Echoes, ripples, buzz'd whispers, love-root, silk-thread, crotch and vine,
My respiration and inspiration, the beating of my heart, the passing of blood and air through my lungs,
The sniff of green leaves and dry leaves, and of the shore and dark-color'd sea-rocks, and of hay in the barn,
The sound of the belch'd words of my voice loos'd to the eddies of the wind,
A few light kisses, a few embraces, a reaching around of arms,
The play of shine and shade on the trees as the supple boughs wag,
The delight alone or in the rush of the streets, or along the fields and hill-sides,
The feeling of health, the full-noon trill, the song of me rising from bed and meeting the sun.

Have you reckon'd a thousand acres much? have you reckon'd the earth much?
Have you practis'd so long to learn to read?
Have you felt so proud to get at the meaning of poems?

Stop this day and night with me, and you shall possess the origin of all poems,
You shall possess the good of the earth and sun--(there are millions of suns left,)
You shall no longer take things at second or third hand, nor look through the eyes of the dead, nor feed on the spectres in books;
You shall not look through my eyes either, nor take things from me,
You shall listen to all sides, and filter them from your self.

Art Lesson for Celebration of Life Month: Pointillism

George Seurat was a 19th century French artist and the originator of pointillism. Pointillism is a form of painting that consists of the use of dots in contrasting colors in certain places where pure color dots become blended in the viewer's eye to form an image. Rather than brush strokes, Seurat felt that this process would make colors powerful and vivid. In his most famous painting "A Sunday on La Grande Jatte — 1884" Seurat used uniform sizes of dots.

Spending an afternoon in the park is a great way to celebrate life. In his painting, Seurat depicted people enjoying an afternoon in the park. The painting is displayed at the Art Institute of Chicago and became the inspiration for the Stephen Sondheim Broadway musical *Sunday in the Park with George*. There are many other ways of celebrating life, such spending time at home with family, preparing a meal, staring at a moonlit sky, observing the miracles of nature and so on. In this lesson, students paint a pointillism scene illustrating a celebration of life.

MATERIALS

Pencils
Acrylic, tempera or gouache paint
Cardboard, heavy paper or canvas
Paper plates, paper cups, Q-tips

PLAN

1. Discuss pointillism.
2. View Seurat's painting "A Sunday on La Grande Jatte — 1884."
3. Look closely at the painting to see the dots of various colors.
4. Google "Seurat up close" in Google Images to see how the dots of various colors combine to make new colors.
5. Change the size of the picture to see how the dots seem to disappear and help form the painting.

DO

1. Think of a scene where people are celebrating life. The scene can contain people, animals, flowers, the ocean, a sunset and so on.
2. Using a pencil, sketch your scene on cardboard, heavy paper or canvas.
3. To paint with dots, do the following:
   a. Squeeze a little bit of each color that works for your scene onto a paper plate or into a paper cup.
   b. Use Q-tips to apply the dots onto your sketch.
   c. Instead of mixing colors, use proximity of dots to create the illusion of color. For example: if you want grass to be different shades of green, apply white dots next to green dots to create lighter areas and black dots next to green dots for darker areas. Dots may overlap.
4. Back your painting with color construction paper and exhibit masterpieces on a bulletin board or around the classroom.

Technology Lesson for Martin Luther King, Jr. Day: Presenting Dr. Martin Luther King, Jr.

In this project, students create a slide show about Dr. Martin Luther King, Jr. As they create their presentations, they will gain an understanding of Dr. King's role in the Civil Rights Movement and gain an appreciation of his significance to American culture and history.

MATERIALS

- Devices with Internet connections
- Multimedia software such as PowerPoint, Keynote, Slides
- Board or chart paper with markers

PLAN

- Students will create a six-page multimedia presentation.
- Write the following headings on a board or chart:
  1. Cover page - Presenting Dr. Martin Luther King, Jr.
  2. The Man
  3. The Civil Rights Movement
  4. The Dream
  5. The Holiday
  6. Civil Rights Today
- During a class discussion, have students share information they know about each of the headings and record their responses.

DO

- Students work in pairs and search the Internet to find information for each of the slide headings listed on the chart or board.
- Students open a new presentation document in the multimedia program of choice and proceed as follows:
  - Create a presentation consisting of six slides.
  - Save the presentation as "Dr. Martin Luther King, Jr." and continue to save often as you go from slide to slide.
  - Design a cover for the presentation.
  - Title the cover slide "Presenting Dr. Martin Luther King, Jr."
  - Select a background and import a graphic to show off the cover.
  - Move to the second slide. Title it "The Man." Research the life of Dr. King. Type what you have learned. Add a background and graphics to the slide. Search the web for an audio clip of a quote from one of his famous speeches. Place it on the slide.
  - Move to the third slide. Title it "The Civil Rights Movement." Research important events in the Civil Rights Movement such as Brown v. Board of Education, the

desegregation of Little Rock, March on Washington. Type what you have learned. Add a background and graphics to the slide.

- Move to the fourth slide. Title it "The Dream." Find a copy of the speech "I Have a Dream" on the Internet. Copy and paste your favorite portion of the text on the card/slide. Add a background and graphics.
- Move to the fifth slide. Title it "The Holiday." Research how the Martin Luther King holiday began and how it is celebrated. Type what you have learned. Add a background and graphics to the slide.
- Move to the sixth slide. Title it "Civil Rights Today." Think about the state of civil rights today compared to the rights 50 years ago. Type your opinion of what has changed for the better and what still needs to change. Add a background and graphics to the slide.
- As time permits, add extra slides, pictures, audios and videos about Dr. King (optional).
- Beginning with the title slide, add transitions, sounds and other actions of your choice to move the viewer through your slide show.
- Save your presentation.
- Present it proudly.

Math Extension for Martin Luther King, Jr. Day: Milestone Math

Using birthdates and milestone timelines, students practice creating and solving multiple step math problems.

MLK, Jr. Milestone Timeline

1/15/1929	1944	1946	1953	1956	1957	1963	1964	1968
Birth	Graduated High School	Graduated College	Married Coretta Scott	Win Bus Boycott	Formed Southern Christian Leadership Conference	Made "I have a Dream Speech"	Youngest recipient the Nobel Piece Prize	Assassinated

MLK's Children's Birthdates

Yolanda Denise ....November 17, 1955
Martin Luther III ....October 23, 1957
Dexter Scott..January 30, 1961
Bernice Albertine ....March 28, 1963

MLK's Parent's Birthdates

Martin Luther "Daddy" King, Sr......................December 19, 1897
Alberta Christine Williams..............................September 13, 1903

1. To begin the lesson, copy and distribute or project the above information.
2. Write the following problem on the board or a chart as an example of a multi-step word problem and have student volunteers determine the solution.
   How many years apart were Martin Luther King, Jr., and his father?
   How old was each at the time Martin Luther King, Jr. won the Nobel Peace Prize?
   Step 1: How old was his dad when Martin was born?
   (1929–1897 = 32)
   Step 2: How old was he when he won the Nobel Peace Prize?
   (1964-1929= 35)
   Step 3: How old was his father when his son won the Nobel Peace Prize?
   His dad's age at his birth plus his age at winning the prize.
   (32 + 35 = 67)
3. Working as a whole class, practice using the data to create and solve a multi-step problem.
4. Divide the class into small groups and have each group write and solve several word problems.
5. Each group will present one problem to the whole class and call on classmates to solve.
6. Culminate the lesson by discussing what students have learned about solving multiple step problems and about the life of Dr. Martin Luther King, Jr.

Poetry Lesson for Martin Luther King, Jr. Day: Hold Fast to Dreams

Like Martin Luther King, Jr., Langston Hughes also believed in the power of dreams. Hughes wrote about the importance of dreams and what happens "when dreams die." In his first stanza of the poem, Hughes describes the desperation of a life without dreams in the metaphor "Life is a broken-winged bird/That cannot fly."

MATERIALS

- Langston Hughes Biography and his poem *Hold Fast to Dreams*
- Word processing or desktop publishing software or pencils, pens, and paper

PLAN

- Read and discuss Langston Hughes's biography.
- Read the poem and explain a metaphor. For example: A metaphor compares two objects to each other without using the words like or as. Hughes compares life without dreams to both a "broken-winged bird" and "a barren field."
- Discuss the following questions:
  - What kind of dreams is Hughes writing about?
  - What does "hold fast" in the title mean?
  - How does he feel about life without dreams?

DO

Getting Ready to Write

During a brainstorming session, ask students to think of sad metaphors to describe life without dreams. For example, *Life without dreams is a clock that cannot tell time.*

Writing the Poem

- Ask students to title their poem "Hold Fast to Dreams" or anything that has a similar meaning.
- Students begin by copying the first two lines of Hughes' poem.
- Begin their third line with "Life is" and their own sad metaphor.
- Students add as many stanzas as they like repeating the steps above.

Editing and Publishing

- Students read a stanza of their poem to the class.
- Students write their poems in a poetry book or enter them in a word processing program.
- Students illustrate their final masterpiece.

Poet Biography for Martin Luther King, Jr. Day
Langston Hughes Biography
February 1, 1902 - May 22, 1967

Langston Hughes began writing poetry in grammar school. When Hughes was growing up, he encountered prejudice not only because he was Black but also because he was part Indian and part white. He achieved recognition as a Black poet. His grandmother always had confidence in his ability to succeed and he did. From the time he was very young, she told him stories about slaves.

After his grandmother died, Hughes went to live with his mother and stepfather. He was elected class poet in grammar school and from that moment on he knew he wanted to be a poet.

Langston was involved in politics and continued to be a social activist throughout his life. He toured the Southern and Southwestern United States, doing readings at black and white universities. He was often upset by the lack of social activism on the part of educated Black people. Hughes continually called for an end to racism and segregation in America. He felt Blacks should not be "secondary Americans." He did not allow himself to be in that position and believed no one of any race should be.

Hughes often said that he wished to give Black children pride in themselves. Many of his poems are directed to children encouraging them to hold on to their dreams no matter what happens. Hughes knew the value of dreams, without which life is empty and nothing changes.

Hold Fast to Dreams
by Langston Hughes

NOTE: *The entire poem is available online. You can search for it online or you can go to the following website and find the poem where it is ready to print, copy, and share with your class.*

http://www.poemhunter.com/poem/dreams-2/

With the use of metaphors, Hughes in his two-stanza poem, *Hold Fast to Dreams*, describes what life is like without dreams. Below are two consecutive lines from the first stanza illustrating one of these metaphors.

> Life is a broken-winged bird
> That cannot fly.

Poetry Lesson for Martin Luther King, Jr. Day: My Country 'Tis of Thee

Samuel Francis Smith wrote the lyrics to the patriotic song *My Country 'Tis of Thee*, also known as *America*. The song was one of our country's unofficial national anthems for nearly one hundred years before the adoption of *The Star-Spangled Banner*. The words "let freedom ring" from this song were quoted in Martin Luther King, Jr.'s famous *I Have a Dream* speech. Dr. King ends his famous speech by giving examples where freedom should ring across this land. In this lesson, students will write their own poems using these famous words.

MATERIALS

- Samuel Francis Smith Biography and his lyrics from the song *My Country 'Tis of Thee*
- Word processing or desktop publishing software or pencils, pens and paper

PLAN

- Read and discuss Samuel Francis Smith's biography and lyrics.
- Discuss the lyrics with the following questions:
  - What does *tis, thee* and *thy* mean?
  - What does Smith love about our country?
  - Where does freedom ring in Smith's song?

DO

Getting Ready to Write

- Play a recording of Dr. King's *I Have a Dream* speech, found on the Internet. Have students listen and write down a few of his references to where he wants freedom to ring. For example, "Let freedom ring from the snow-capped Rockies of Colorado."
- Students share what they have heard and written.
- In a class discussion, elicit student responses to where freedom should ring that are both concrete and poetic.
  For example, concrete places like: *from the mountains, from the wheat fields of Kansas*
- For poetic responses, prompt students to come up with examples that are not places.
  For example: *from every bird's song, from the lips of a child, from the breeze twirling through the trees*

Writing the Poem

Students write poems of their own using "let freedom ring" as a springboard. Encourage line breaks so that the poem looks like a poem and not like a story.

- Suggest students title their poems "Let Freedom Ring."
- Begin the first line of the poem with the words "Let freedom ring."
- The second line describes from where they want freedom to ring and begins with the word "From."
- Continue each line with "From" and write other examples of where they want freedom to ring.
- Students end their poem by repeating the line "Let freedom ring."

Editing and Publishing

- Students read and edit poems with partners.
- Students sing the song and read their poems.

Poet Biography for Martin Luther King, Jr. Day
Samuel Frances Smith Biography
October 21, 1808 - November 16, 1895

Samuel Frances Smith was born in Boston, Massachusetts. He attended Harvard College, now known as Harvard University, and graduated in 1829. After graduating Harvard, he went to Andover Seminary School. While there he supported himself by accepting literary work. He was asked to translate some German verses including a patriotic hymn. After reading this stirring hymn, he knew that the United States needed its own patriotic national poem. He wrote *America*, which was to become *My Country 'Tis of Thee*, on scraps of paper. This famous poem was written in less than thirty minutes.

Five months after its completion, this song made its debut. A children's choir in Boston sang it in a church on Independence Day in 1831 and the song became instantly popular. One leader at the school was quoted as saying "Every crisis will hear it above the storm." The lyrics were original, whereas the melody was the official national melody of at least twenty other nations.

In 1834, Smith married Mary White. They had six children. In that same year he also became ordained as a Baptist minister in Maine and a professor of modern languages at Waterville College. He left Maine and went to Newton, Massachusetts where he became editor of several Christian publications and pastor of a Baptist church.

From 1875 through 1880, he traveled to Europe and Asia to missionary outposts. He easily learned languages and was accomplished in fifteen different languages in his lifetime. In 1893, two years before his death, he was a potential candidate for an honorary Doctor of Letters degree from Harvard University. However, the university's president declined, saying that *My Country 'Tis of Thee* is better known for its melody than its words. Smith wrote over 150 hymns over the years. His most famous, *My Country 'Tis of Thee*, will be remembered by patriots for hundreds of years to come.

On November 16, 1895, while on a train to preach in Boston, Smith died. At his funeral with his wife and five of his children attending, *My Country 'Tis of Thee* was one of the pieces sung. Sixty-eight years after his death, Dr. Martin Luther King, Jr. quoted the first verse of *My Country 'Tis of Thee* in his famous *I Have a Dream* speech.

My Country 'Tis of Thee
by Samuel Frances Smith

My country, 'tis of thee,
Sweet land of liberty,
Of thee I sing;
Land where my fathers died,
Land of the pilgrims' pride,
From every mountainside,
Let freedom ring!

My native country, thee,
Land of the noble free,
Thy name I love;
I love thy rocks and rills,
Thy woods and templed hills;
My heart with rapture thrills,
Like that above.

Let music swell the breeze,
And ring from all the trees,
Sweet freedom's song;
Let mortal tongues awake;
Let all that breathe partake;
Let rocks their silence break,
The sound prolong.

Our fathers' God, to Thee,
Author of liberty,
To Thee we sing;
Long may our land be bright
With freedom's holy light;
Protect us by Thy might,
Great God, our King.

Engineering Lesson for International Thank You Day: Assembly Line Thank You Notes

International Thank You Day is a day to say thank you to friends, family and other people in your life who have taught you, helped you, brightened your day and made your neighborhood, country and the world a better place. In this lesson, student groups will create a design for thank you notes to be produced using a manufacturing process called progressive assembly also known as an assembly line. Once the group gathers materials and decides on a design, it will work together to create the individual parts for the cards. When the parts are completed, each group member will be responsible for adding one part of the card in sequence as they move the card across the newly-created assembly line until the final card is produced. The goal of each group will be to produce as many cards as possible during the time period allowed (usually 20 to 30 minutes).

MATERIALS

- 8 1/2 x 5 1/2 white card stock (cut 8 1/2 x 11 in half to create the size)
- Colored paper, 5 x 7 greeting card envelopes
- Rulers, scissors, glue
- Pencils, paper, felt-tip pens
- Board or chart paper
- Assortment of decorating materials (possible list below):
  1. Stickers
  2. Patterned sticky tape
  3. Ribbons and bows
  4. Patterned paper and wrapping paper
  5. Colored dots
  6. Press on gems such as sequins
  7. Artificial flowers

PLAN

- During a class discussion, talk about International Thank You Day, the purpose of which is to show appreciation by saying thank you to people who make your life better.
- Tell students that the class is going to make thank you cards to distribute throughout the day.
- Students create a class list of people they would like to thank today. For example: school bus drivers, gardeners, crossing guards, friends, teachers and other school personnel, family, etc. Write their responses on the board or chart.
- Explain the concept of an assembly line and demonstrate how a card making assembly line works. Have five volunteers come up to create a very simple thank you card in assembly line style by following the steps on the next page.
- Explain that once the process begins, it keeps going so that many cards can be produced in a short amount of time.

- Supplies needed for the demonstration are: 5 1/2 x 11 white card stock, felt tip pens, stickers, crayons and envelopes.
  1. First student folds white card stock in half horizontally and scores it with a ruler to make the fold sharp and then passes it to the second student.
  2. Second student uses a felt-tip pen to write "Thank You" on the pre-cut strip of colored paper, pastes it on the card and passes it to the next student.
  3. Third student decorates the card with stickers and passes it to the next student.
  4. Fourth student draws a simple design or picture on the card using colored pencils or crayons and passes it to the next student
  5. Fifth student places the card in the envelope and puts the envelope in a box.

DO

- Divide the class into groups of five.
- Display items that can be used to create cards on a table in the room.
- Have each group walk around the table to see what supplies are available without taking any.
- Have the groups return to their area and plan the card they will create as follows:
  1. List the materials they will need.
  2. Write a step-by step plan for creating the card.
  3. Identify who is going to perform each task.
  4. Each group gathers the materials needed, places them in order in assembly line fashion and assembles the cards.
- The finished cards are divided among the group members to be distributed as Thank You Day cards.
- During a group evaluation, members decide how they would improve their assembly line in the future.

2nd grade classroom

Science Extension for International Thank You Day: Thank You Solar Advocates

January 11th is International Thank You Day. In this lesson students gain background knowledge about solar energy, build a solar oven to make s'mores, observe the sun at work and celebrate the holiday by showing gratitude to people who are innovators in solar energy.

MATERIALS

- S'mores Solar Oven Supplies
  - Four empty large pizza boxes
  - Black construction paper
  - Aluminum foil
  - Box cutters, scissors
  - Clear plastic wrap
  - Glue and tape
  - Rulers, pen or pencils
  - Wooden skewers
  - Chocolate bars, graham crackers, and mini marshmallows

- Thank You Notes Supplies
  - Digital device for email letters
  - Paper, envelopes, stamps for snail mail letters
  - Solar Scientists Thank You Letters Handout

WHAT IS SOLAR POWER?

Place the following terms on the board or chart. Discuss each term with the class and write student responses next to each word. The words below are written with definitions for help in guiding the discussion.

a. renewable energy
   energy from a source that is not depleted when used, such as wind or solar power
b. solar energy
   relates to or denotes energy harvested from the sun's rays and converted into electricity
c. solar cells
   tools that change light energy from the sun and other light sources into electricity, for example many calculators use solar cells for power
d. solar panel
   a group of solar cells connected to form a large, flat surface

Discuss how a solar oven works. During the month of January, your solar oven experiments will only work on sunny days. The ideal outdoor temperature for a solar oven is at least 70 degrees. Anything cooler, will take longer to bake.

BUILDING A SOLAR OVEN

Divide the class into four groups. Have each group build a solar oven out of an empty pizza box and bake s'mores.

1. Use a ruler and a marker to measure and draw a two-inch border on the top of a closed pizza box.
2. Use a box cutter (depending upon the age of your students you may wish to cut the boxes), cut along the front line and the lines on the sides of the box. Leave the line at the back uncut. Using the remaining line as a guide, fold back the top of the box to create a flap.
3. Measure and cut two pieces of aluminum foil. Measure the first piece to fit on the underside of the flap. Measure the second piece to line the entire inside of the box including the sides. Glue both pieces into place.
4. Create an oven window by securely taping and sealing the plastic wrap to the underside of the cut opening at the top of the box.
5. Place and glue a sheet of black construction paper to the bottom of the inside of the box on top of the foil.
6. Wrap a thin piece of tape to the skewer and tape it to the top of the box to create a kick-stand for the lid.

MAKING THE S'MORES

1. Bring the ovens, chocolate bars, marshmallows and graham crackers outside on the sunniest day possible.
2. Place the ovens to best capture the sunlight. Make sure the inside flap is facing the sun. If January in your area has no sun, use a sun lamp.
3. Have groups rotate members so that the progress of the cooking is watched at several time intervals.
4. When the s'mores are ready, enjoy!

THANK YOU LETTERS TO SOLAR POWER ADVOCATES

1. Distribute Thank You Letter Handouts.
2. Students work in pairs or individually following the directions on the handout.
3. Students write snail mail letters, address and stamp envelopes using the school address and classroom number as their return address.
4. The letters are mailed.

Solar Scientists Thank You Letters Handout

Celebrate International Thank You Day by writing thank you letters to people who are making a difference promoting and using solar power. Below are a few names and contact information to get you started. Write the letter to one of the people listed or a person you know who has embraced the use of solar power. Begin your letter with an initial sentence thanking them. Tell about yourself and how important their support is to you. Include how the growing use of alternative fuels such as solar power will affect your life, the life of future generations and the world environment. Include what your dreams are for the future. If you wish to receive a response, ask them questions and tell them how to respond to you (your school snail mail, your school email address, etc.).

Elon Musk is the CEO of Tesla Motors and SpaceX. He has been a champion for the incredible potential of renewable energy. Musk, at the American Geophysical Union in San Francisco, said "the U.S. could meet its electricity needs just by covering a small corner of Utah or Nevada with solar panels." Research more of Musk's work for further information. Send a letter by snail mail to Elon Musk at the following address: Space Exploration Technologies, Attn: Elon Musk, 1 Rocket Road, Hawthorne, CA 90250

Leonardo DiCaprio is an actor and producer who founded the Leo DiCaprio Foundation that is dedicated to the long-term health and wellbeing of all Earth's inhabitants. DiCaprio's foundation places particular emphasis on the issues of alternative and renewable energy sources, and the preservation of biodiversity. He even used solar energy to power the set of his thriller movie, Inception. Send a letter to:
Leonardo DiCaprio c/o Appian Way Productions, 9255 Sunset Blvd., Suite 615,
West Hollywood, CA 90069

Bill Nye the Science Guy is a supporter of alternative energy and climate science. He has several YouTube videos and online posts on the positive uses of solar energy. He is quoted as saying, "I hope climate science becomes the big thing. And then what I want is electrical engineers to solve the world's energy problems, energy distribution problems. I want mechanical engineers to make better transportation systems. I want chemical engineers to develop better solar panels, and so on." Send a letter to:
Bill Nye c/o The Planetary Society, 60 S Los Robles Ave, Pasadena, CA 91101

Katherine Lucey is a former investment banker with expertise in the energy sector. She is the founder of Solar Sister, a network of entrepreneurial women in rural Africa, who sell clean energy solutions to their communities. In addition to creating access to safe, affordable and clean energy the women earn a steady income to support their families. Learn more about the organization at www.solarsister.org.
Send a letter to Katherine Lucey c/o Solar Sisters Uganda, 251 Kyebando - Kisalosalo Rd, Kampala, Uganda

Mike Strizki is an inventor who founded the Hydrogen House Project dedicated to the pursuit of clean and renewable solutions to help meet the world's increasing energy demand. He conducts research on hydrogen and other clean energy technologies. He retrofitted his house in Hopewell, New Jersey to convert solar energy into hydrogen gas. Actor Johnny Depp hired Mr. Strizki to transform his personal island into a self-sustained oasis of renewable energy that runs on hydrogen solar cells. Send a letter to:
Mike Strizki, Hydrogen House Project, 26 Snydertown Rd, Hopewell, NJ, 08525 USA

Cate Blanchett and her husband Andrew Upton are co-artistic directors of the Sydney Theater Company. They were key proponents of Greening the Wharf, a project that oversaw the installation of 1,900 solar panels on the roof of The Wharf Theatre at Sydney's Walsh Bay. This now provides 70 percent of the theater's energy requirements. Together with a system for rainwater harvesting, the theater will eventually be fully carbon neutral. Under her guidance, the theater also started reusing and recycling costumes and props. Send a letter to:
Kate Blanchett c/o her agent at the following address:
Robyn Gardiner, RGM Associates, P.O. Box 128, Surry Hills NSW, 2010, Australia

"I'd put my money on the sun and solar energy."
Thomas Edison

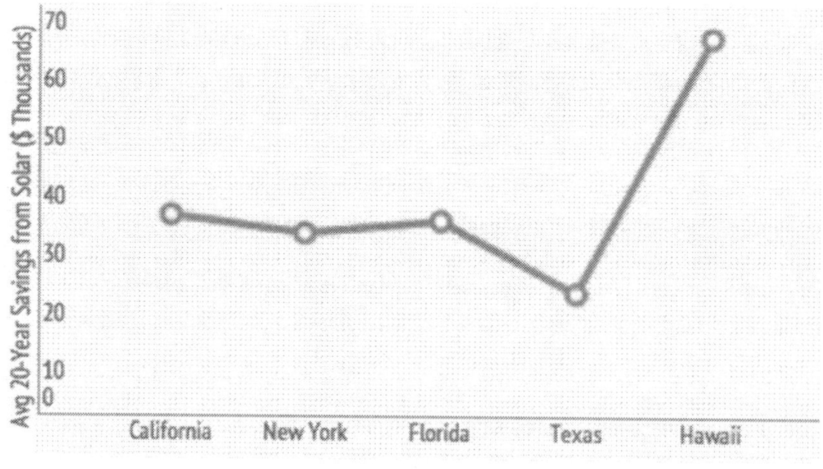

20-Year Savings From Solar (Average)

Poetry Lesson for International Thank You Day: Thanksgiving (A poem for everyday)

It may be January, but Ralph Waldo Emerson's poem *Thanksgiving* is truly a poem for all months. He reminds us to give thanks to people and to everything that enhances our lives, "For rest and shelter of the night,/For health and food,/For love and friends."

MATERIALS

- Ralph Waldo Emerson Biography and his poem *Thanksgiving*
- Word processing or desktop publishing software or pencils, pens and paper, fancy stationery or art materials to create stationery

PLAN

Read and discuss Emerson's biography and poem with sample guiding questions including:

- To what does Emerson think we should give thanks?
- Who is "thy"?

DO

Getting Ready to Write

During a brainstorming session, ask students the following questions. As the class gives their responses, list them on the board or on a chart.

- Emerson is thankful for "each new morning." What are you thankful for in your life?
- To whom would you give thanks?

Writing the Poem

- Suggest students title their poem *Thanksgiving.*
- Have them begin each line with "For" and to whatever and whomever in their everyday life they give thanks.
- Suggest they use line breaks just as Emerson did.

Editing and Publishing

- Students embellish their poem with a fancy border and print.
- Create a display of the finished poems.

International Thank You Day

Poet Biography for International Thank You Day
Ralph Waldo Emerson Biography
May 25, 1803 - April 22, 1882

Ralph Waldo Emerson, who became one of the greatest of all American writers, was born in Concord, MA. By the time Ralph was a year old, he could talk. When he was three years old, he began working at jobs around the house. He was either in school or working. His father was very strict and never showed any affection or love for Ralph or his three brothers. He was a serious little boy, but his aunt thought that he was lazy, loving to read storybooks and recite poems rather than doing the lessons assigned to him. When his father died, his family became very poor. He and one of his brothers, having only one sweater between them, had to trade off wearing it. Other children would laugh at them.

By the time Ralph was nine, he began writing poetry and spent the little spare time he had writing. Ralph and one of his brothers went to live with their mother at their grandparents' home in Concord. He loved the farm in Concord where there was a river for swimming and boating. Climbing the hills and listening to the birds gave him great enjoyment. It was here that he developed a love of nature that would remain with him all of his life. At Harvard College, Ralph was a mediocre student but loved literature. Rather than loving sports, he loved to write in a journal where he also played games with words. He graduated as class poet.

His passion was writing but he presented lectures to make a living. He traveled all over the United States and England. He always spoke to a full house, to both the very educated and the uneducated. The audience came away from his lectures uplifted.

When Ralph grew older, one of his greatest joys was showing love for his children and grandchildren, always remembering his hard childhood and being grateful that it was over. Emerson was a man with magical qualities. He spoke and wrote about the relationships of the spirit with nature and with man's goodness. The goodness that he wrote and lectured about was the goodness that comes from within. Those who knew him well and those that saw him speak considered him an angel.

Thanksgiving
by Ralph Waldo Emerson

For each new morning with its light,
For rest and shelter of the night,
For health and food,
For love and friends,
For everything Thy goodness sends.

For the stars that light the night sky
Noah
2nd grade

For the last drop of water that we drink
Morgan
2nd grade

Art Lesson for International Thank You Day
Marbleizing Paper

Part of the appeal of marbled paper is that each design is unique. To celebrate International Thank You Day, students make their own marbleized paper and write thank you cards to important people in their lives.

Students make marbleized paper floating different patterns of food coloring on the surface of water to which oil is added. Using combs, feathers or other objects, students move the drops of color to form patterns. The patterns are then transferred to paper.

This art form began as early as the 10th century in China. Marbled papers in Turkey have survived from the 14th century. They were used for important documents and for decoration. Marbled papers became popular in Europe in the 17th century. Collected by European travelers to the Middle East, the paper was used for books of friendship that today are similar to autograph albums. Europeans marbleized paper for book covers, drawer linings and book end papers, all of which remain popular today.

MATERIALS

Shallow pans shallow baking or roasting pan, (about 9" x 13" x 2"), one per group
Food coloring or liquid watercolors
3 tbsp. cooking oil per pan
Paper
Eye droppers
Feathers, toothpicks, forks, combs and/or popsicle sticks
Paper

1. Divide the class into small groups (maximum 5 per group).
2. Distribute the materials.
3. Put enough water to cover the bottom of the pans.
4. Mix the oil into the water.
5. Each student takes a turn and does the following:
    a. Picks colors and with a dropper puts the colors on top of the prepared water.
    b. Moves the color drops with a comb or other object to make marbled patterns.
    c. Places paper on the water when the pattern is appealing.
    d. Waits about 30 seconds and gently peels the paper from the water.
    e. Lets the marbleized papers dry.

CONSTRUCTING THE MARBLEIZED THANK YOU NOTES

MATERIALS
Marbled paper
Pens or pencils
Colored markers, crayons
Sequins, stickers, buttons, sticky notes, other decorative materials

1. Fold the marbled paper in half.
2. Write "Thank You" on the front cover in attractive lettering.
3. Decorate the card.
4. Write a thank you message inside the card.
5. Share thank you notes with class.
6. Deliver their notes to the appropriate person.

Mathematics Lesson for New Year's Day: Calendar Challenge

The New Year's Mathematics Calendar Challenge is an excellent activity in which to review math concepts to get ready for new learning in the coming year. In this project-based activity, student groups create word problems using the days and weeks of the month.

MATERIALS

- January calendar page
- Pencils
- Projector
- Chart Paper

PLAN

- Project the calendar page for January on the board.
- Using calendar information, guide the class as they create one or two math questions about concepts they have learned. Write the problems and their solutions on the chart.
- The following are examples from the January 2017 calendar page:
    1. Multiply the date of the fourth Wednesday in January by the fraction created by using the date of the first Thursday in January as the numerator and the fourth Wednesday in January as the denominator. Answer: 25 x 5/25 = 25 x 1/5 = 5
    2. Write the numerals for the first five days in the second week of January (beginning on Sunday) in sequential order. Place commas where they belong and write the word name of the created numeral.
       Answer: 89,101,112
       Eighty-nine million, one hundred one thousand, one hundred twelve

DO

- Divide the class into small groups.
- Distribute a January calendar page to each group.
- Using the calendar, have each group write several challenging math problems and their solutions.
- Have student volunteers from each group write one or two of the problems their group has created on chart paper for the rest of the class to solve.

Engineering Extension for New Year's Day
New Year's Mandala

Mandala is the Sanskrit word that roughly means circle. The art encompassed in the mandala stems from Buddhist and Hindu traditions. Spiritual leaders often used mandalas as a tool to strengthen meditation and increase focus. In this lesson student engineers create mandalas to express plans for entering the next year with focus and creativity.

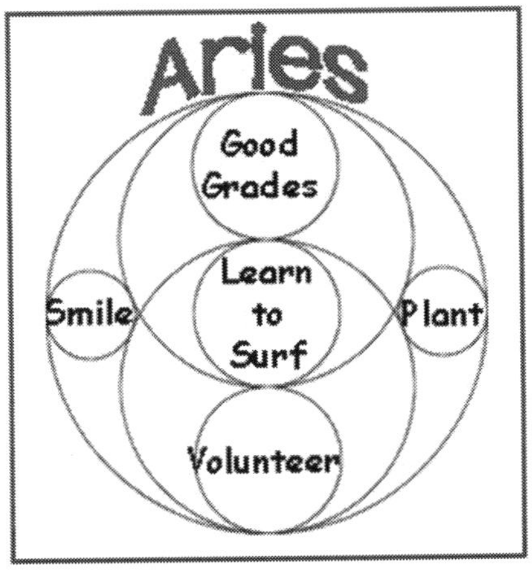

MATERIALS

10" paper plates
Glue, scissors
Markers, watercolors, pastels, colored pencils
Assortment of textured and colored paper
Houses of the Zodiac Handout
Mandala Template Handout

PLAN

Download traditional mandala pictures from the Internet. Discuss the origin and current uses of mandalas as follows:

The name "Mandala" comes from the Sanskrit word that means circle.

a. The art of the traditional mandala stems from Buddhist and Hindu traditions.
b. Today the mandala has become a common term for a variety of diagrams and geometric patterns that are designed for self-reflection as well as reflection on nature and the universe.

1. Students create a New Year Mandala based on the twelve houses of the zodiac.
2. Distribute the Houses of the Zodiac Handout and discuss.
3. Have students work in groups of two, three or four and brainstorm items to include in each category of the Zodiac Handout.

DO

1. Distribute the Mandala Template Handout, 10" paper plates, glue, art supplies and paper assortment.
2. Have students create their New Year's Mandalas as follows:
   a. Cut out the Mandala Template and paste it onto a 10" paper plate.
   b. Write the name of a different house of the zodiac in a clock like pattern above each of the twelve sections. Begin writing the name Aries in the one o'clock section and end with Pisces in the section at 12 o'clock.
   c. Write the goal for each house of the zodiac somewhere in each section.
   d. Plan the design the mandala using words, symbols, and shapes.
   e. Evaluate the plan and make any necessary modifications.
   f. Create the mandala using a variety of art supplies and colored papers.
   g. Share mandalas with the class.

Houses of the Zodiac Handout

Zodiac	House	Categories
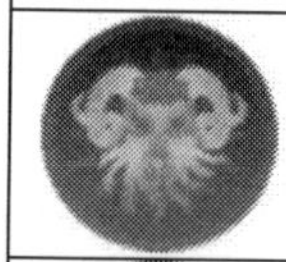	Aries	New beginnings, new projects, inspiration
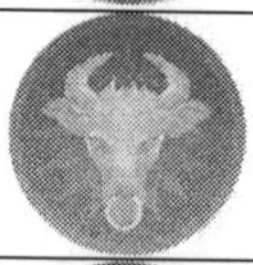	Taurus	Success, material wealth, physical health
	Gemini	Communication, learning
	Cancer	Relationship with self and others
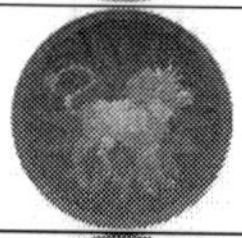	Leo	Art, free will, creativity, love
	Virgo	Organizations, work, family
	Libra	Harmony, balance, relationships
	Scorpio	Money matters, transactions
	Sagitarius	Spirituality, travel, freedom
	Capricorn	Power, dreams, goals, reputation
	Aquarius	Innovations, community
	Pisces	Learning journeys, psychological health

Mandala Template Handout

Poetry Lesson for New Year's Day: New Year

In her poem, Ella Wheeler Wilcox personifies the New Year as she looks "straight into its eyes." Throughout the poem she tells the New Year that because of her positive perspective, strength and courage, she can help make it a good year.

MATERIALS

- Ella Wheeler Wilcox Biography and her poem *New Year*
- Word processing or desktop publishing software or pencils, pens, and paper

PLAN

Read and discuss Wilcox's biography and poem. Some sample guiding questions include:

- Where does Wilcox use personification?
- What does the New Year look like when she first sees it?
- Is she concerned about what this New Year will bring?
- How does she think she can make it a good New Year?

DO

Getting Ready to Write

During a brainstorming session, ask students the following questions:

- Using personification how would you begin talking to the New Year?
- What kind of person do you picture the New Year to be?
- What actions would you take to make the New Year a good one?

Writing the Poem

- Begin poems by greeting the New Year.
- Describe the New Year.
- Tell the New Year how you plan to make it a good year.
- Use powerful and descriptive parts of speech.

Editing and Publishing

- Have students read and edit poems with partners.
- Have students write their poems in a poetry book or enter them in a word processing program.
- Illustrate their final masterpiece.

Poet Biography for New Year's Day
Ella Wheeler Wilcox Biography
November 5, 1850 - October 30, 1919

Ella Wheeler Wilcox was born in Wisconsin. She was raised in an environment that nurtured her poetic talent. Her mother and many of her aunts and cousins wrote poetry and she was introduced to great works of literature.

At a young age, she began to write poems. Her writing was well known in Wisconsin before she had even graduated from high school. She was an optimistic person and most of her poetry expresses that optimism. One of her most famous poems begins with the lines "Laugh, and the world laughs with you;/Weep, and you weep alone."

At age 34 she married Robert Wilcox. They loved to have gatherings in their home in Long Island where they entertained literary and artistic people. They had one son who died at a very young age. She and her husband were spiritual people. They remained married until his death.

One of her brothers said, "She wrote for the same reason that a bird sings. It was what she was made for." Wilcox became a well-known poet and a writer of quotes. In the opening of the movie JFK directed by Oliver Stone, she is quoted, "To sin by silence when we should protest makes cowards out of men." The first stanza of her poem titled "The Man Worth While" can be seen in Disney's Hollywood Studios. The first four lines describe how Ella Wheeler Wilcox lived her life and how she encouraged others with her optimistic and brave view:

> "It is easy enough to be pleasant
> When life flows by like a song,
> But the man worthwhile is the one who will smile
> When everything goes dead wrong."

New Year
by Ella Wheeler Wilcox

New Year, I look straight in your eyes –
Our ways and our interests blend;
You may be a foe in disguise,
But I shall believe you a friend.
We get what we give in our measure,
We cannot give pain and get pleasure;
I give you good will and good cheer,
And you must return it, New Year.

We get what we give in this life,
Though often the giver indeed
Waits long upon doubting and strife
Ere proving the truth of my creed.
But somewhere, some way, and forever
Reward is the meed of endeavour;
And if I am really worth while,
New Year, you will give me your smile.

You hide in your mystical hand
No "luck" that I cannot control,
If I trust my own courage and stand
On the Infinite strength of my soul.
Man holds in his brain and his spirit
A power that is God-like, or near it,
And he who has measured his force
Can govern events and their course.

You come with a crown on your brow,
New Year, without blemish or spot;
Yet you, and not I, sir, must bow,
For time is the servant of thought
Whatever you bring me of trouble
Shall turn into good, and then double,
If my spirit looks up without fear
To the Source that you came from, New Year.

Photography Lesson: Photography for a New Year Calendar

In this lesson, student photographers use smartphones, tablets, disposable cameras and/or digital cameras to take a series of photos. They place their favorite photo or photos on yearly calendars created by using templates from their favorite spreadsheet program. Since most of these cameras do not have the technical or editing powers of more sophisticated cameras, the composition of the photos taken is of utmost importance. The elements of composition students focus on are: color, light, line and space.

1. Students learn important elements necessary for taking good pictures and put this knowledge to use. They place their favorite shots on photo calendars for the New Year.

2. Find photographs from the Internet, books and/or magazines and project. Discuss the following elements of composition: color, light, line and space. These elements are crucial for composing good photographs.

   a. Color – The colors in a photograph are often chosen to evoke different feelings. Two general categories of color are cool and warm. The cool colors are those on the blue-green spectrum. Cool colors bring about tranquil feelings of peace and calm. Warm colors are reds, yellows and oranges. These colors arouse feelings of excitement and happiness. They are often used in billboards and logos. In this photo, taken by an astronaut, the colors of the American Flag contrast with the soft colors of the moon.

   b. Line – The lines in a photograph can be very powerful. The viewer's eyes will follow a line to the subject of the photo.
   A photographer can draw the viewer to look at a subject by placing the subject at the end of a line. An excellent photo to illustrate the effect of lines in a photograph is Henri Cartier Bresson's Photo - *Hyeres, France 1932.*

c. Light – Light has an important effect on the way a photo looks. The same scene photographed facing towards the sun, away from the sun, at different times of the day, or on sunny or overcast days, can look very different from one another. Like lines, light can also direct the user's eyes towards a subject. Our eyes tend to first focus on the most brightly lit part of a scene. This photo taken in 1932 by Lewis Hine, *Worker on the Empire State Building,* is a good example of the use of light to focus on a subject.

d. Space – Leaving empty or negative space around the subject of a photo causes the subject to stand out. Photographers often use the sky as negative space. Check that no other elements or objects in your photo draws the eye away from your subject.

3. Students use available smartphones, tablets, disposable cameras and/or digital cameras to take a series of photos paying attention to the elements of composition they have discussed.

4. Students select one of their photographs to include in a yearly photo calendar. Create a calendar in a variety of programs, for example, a template in your favorite word processing or spreadsheet program. There are calendar templates in PrintShop and on-line calendar creators. There are also a variety of printing companies including Shutterfly, Snapfish, VistaPrint and more that offer calendar templates.

February Monthly Holidays

American Heart Month • Black History Month • National Canned Food Month • Celebration of Chocolate Month • Great American Pies Month • Human Relations Month • International Embroidery Month • National Cherry Month • National Children's Dental Month • Potato Lover's Month • Return Shopping Carts to the Supermarket Month

February Weekly Holidays

First Week of February
National Pay Your Bills Week

Second Week of February
Boy Scouts Week • National Crime Prevention Week • Big Brothers/Big Sisters Week • Laughter Keeps Us From Getting Dizzy Week

Third Week of February
National Brotherhood Week • International Friendship Week

Last Week of February
Pancake Week

February Moveable Holidays

Clean Out Your Computer Day..........second Monday

Race Relations Sunday .... Sunday nearest February 12

President's Day..........third Monday

Chinese New Year..........Second new moon after the Winter Solstice

Chinese Lantern Festival Day..........Fourteen days
..........after Chinese New Year

February Days for STEM Makers and Poets

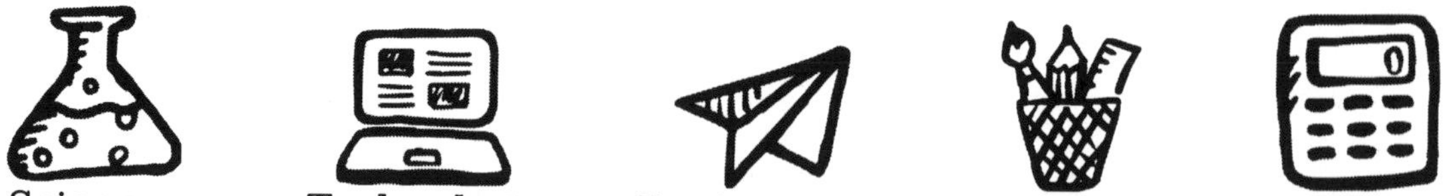

		Day	Make and Do
1		Hula in the Coola Day	For those in cold climates, Hula in the Coola Day comes just in time to warm your chilly bones. Your job is to plan a hula party with grass skirts, coconut shells and all things tropical. What games will you play? What tropical food will you serve? Create an invitation for your party.
2		Groundhog Day	Punxsutawney Phil may or may not see his shadow today, but if you have sunshine go outside and draw shadows. Measure and record a classmate's shadow with chalk in the morning and before lunch. What time was your shadow the longest and what time was it the shortest? Observe and record the position of the sun at each time.
3		Elmo's Birthday	Find your way to Sesame Street and wish Elmo a happy birthday. Make an Elmo sculpture out of red playdough that you make yourself. Mix ½ cup salt, q/2 cup water and 1 cup flour. Add in red food dye (not the gel kind, it stains). You can add a little oil if you like. Adjust with more flour or more water to get the right consistency.
4		Midpoint Day	Celebrate winter's midpoint today. We are halfway to spring. Make a list of ten midpoint questions with ten answers. For example, when is the midpoint of the school year? Be sure and answer in complete sentences.

5		Bubble Gum Day	Bubble Gum Day is a day of fun, learning and charitable giving. At participating schools, everyone who donates 50 cents or more gets to chew gum in school. Incorporate bubblegum into your day. In science class, unwrap a piece of gum and weigh it. After chewing for five minutes, has the weight changed? Why? In math, practice estimation. How many gumballs will fill a container?
6		Mary Leakey's Birthday	Mary Leakey, the "Grande Dame of Archeology," was born on this day in 1913. She along with husband Louis Leakey became one of science's best known married teams. They discovered a skull fossil of an ancestor of apes and humans in 1960 that helped us learn more about the origins of man. Write a short biography of Mary Leakey highlighting her contributions to science.
7		National Periodic Table Day	Early man, prior to the 1st century A.D., knew just a few elements including gold, silver, lead, tin, mercury, carbon and sulfur. On this day in 1863, chemist John Newlands, published the known 56 elements into a table, each arranged by their atomic weight. There have been very few significant changes in the 20th century. The Periodic Table remains one of the most important tools in chemistry. Print out a periodic table and create a board game or a battleship game to learn the elements.
8		National Kite Flying Day	Let's go fly a kite! Kites date back to Ancient China over 3,000 years ago. Download the American Kitefliers Association's "Kites in the Classroom" at http://aka.kite.org/docs/Manuals/kitc.pdf for many ideas that integrate kites into science, math and art. You can build a kite in less than thirty minutes. Visit www.instructables.com and search for "easy paper kites for kids" to find supplies needed and directions.

9		National Toothache Day	This annual observance may be connected to the founding of Hershey chocolate in 1894. What causes a toothache? See if your local dentist will come to your class and show you what happens when you place a tooth in a cola drink.
10		Plimsoll Day	In 1876, Samuel Plimsoll was instrumental in assuring that ships were not dangerously overloaded by adding legislation in the English Parliament. He has since earned the moniker "sailor's friend." The Plimsoll line (the water line) marks the depth at which a ship can be loaded. The line varies with the kind of water and the time of year. Ships float lower in freshwater than in saltwater because saltwater is denser than freshwater. Try floating an object in both kinds of water and draw the Plimsoll line for each.
11		National Inventor's Day	In 1983, President Reagan designated February 11 as National Inventor's Day in honor of Thomas Edison's birthday and to recognize the enormous contribution made by inventors to the nation and the world." Create a "Gallery of Inventors" multimedia presentation. Have students work in teams to make a group presentation. Students can contribute to the group presentation by sharing information about the inventor of their choice.
12		National Lost Penny Day	Lincoln, our 16th president, was born on this day in 1809. Lincoln is immortalized on the penny, so it is only fitting in honor of this great man that we celebrate Lost Penny Day. The first US penny was made of pure copper and minted in 1787. In 1909, to mark the 100th anniversary of Lincoln's birth, the U.S. mint debuted the first Lincoln penny. For one week, search, gather and count all the lost pennies you can find and donate them to a favorite charity. Did you know that it costs 1.67 cents to make a penny?

13		World Radio Day	This day is hosted by UNESCO (The United Nations Education, Scientific and Cultural Organization). World Radio Day encourages radio broadcasters to promote information access, freedom of expression, gender equality and empowerment of women. Everyone has a story to tell. With a smart phone or other recording device, create a radio show. Check out Shout Out: A Kid's Guide to Recording Stories at http://transom.org/2013/katie-davis-kids-guide-recording/ to get going.
14		Have a Heart Day	It's Valentine's Day, and the perfect day to celebrate by learning about heart-healthy food choices. What makes a heart-healthy menu? Begin by searching the American Heart Association website. Keep a food diary by listing everything you eat for a day and summarize your food intake on a chart. Categories include: fruit, dairy, vegetables, bread/cereal/pasta, lean meat and fats/oils/sweets. Which foods are "everyday foods" and which are "sometimes foods?" Analyze how you could make your choices heart-healthy. Write a paragraph to go with your chart.
15		National Gumdrop Day	Gumdrops look great on gingerbread houses, but today is reserved for some tasty gumdrop engineering. With 25 toothpicks and 11 gumdrops, build a geodesic dome (just like EPCOT). You will find complete directions at the Scientific American website found at: http://www.scientificamerican.com/artic le/sphere-based-science-build-your-own-geodesic-dome/

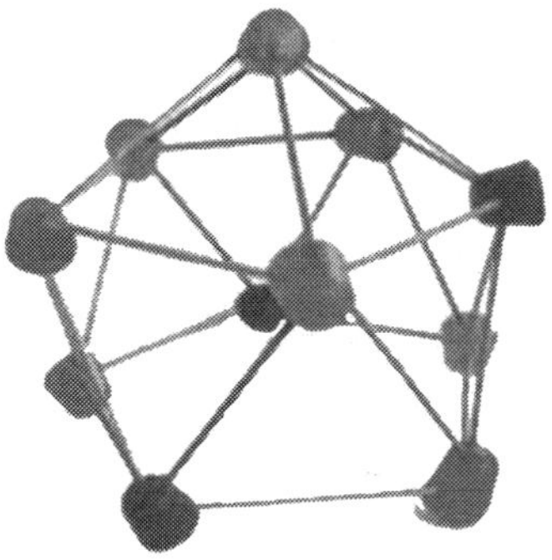

16		National Almond Day	Go nuts today! Almonds are both seeds and super foods. They date back to ancient times. Make some almond milk art. Pour almond milk in the bottom of a tray and place dots of food coloring on the surface of the milk. Add small drops of dishwashing soap. Watch the colors twist and twirl as the soap molecules cause a reaction with the fat molecules in the almond milk. Quickly dip a piece of paper in the mixture to preserve your work of art.
17		The Volkswagen Beetle Beats Ford	On this day in 1972, Volkwagen produced its 15,007,034th Beetle, surpassing Ford's Model T as the most produced car in history. The Beetle came to America in the 1950s. The ad campaigns helped sales. In 1959, their ad read "Think Small" at a time when large cars were the norm. Find several ads used to sell the Beetle on the Internet. What do you notice about the ads? What slogans did they use? Choose your favorite car and write an ad in the style of the VW ads.
18		National Battery Day	Get energized on National Battery Day. Batteries convert chemical energy into electrical energy. Construct a simple circuit with a battery, a bulb and two insulated copper wires. Remove the insulation from the two ends and connect one to the negative end of the battery and one to the positive end. Light up the bulb. Add more batteries and wire. Document what happens.
19		Birthday of Nicolaus Copernicus	Born on this day in 1473, Copernicus revolutionized scientific thought with the theory that the earth revolved around the sun and was not the center of the universe. Research the interesting life of Copernicus. Write a short biography and illustrate with pictures.

20	 	Metropolitan Museum of Art	The Met is the largest art museum in the United States. The museum opened on this day in 1880. Take a virtual tour of the museum at http://www.metmuseum.org. Work with a group to create a presentation about its collections. Use a presentation program. How will you organize your project? Create hotlinks to web information and interactive buttons within your project to create added interest.
21		Introduce a Girl to Engineering Day	Today we highlight careers for women in engineering and encourage them to become creative problem solvers. Have fun doing grade-specific, hands-on engineering activities at your school. Invite professors and engineers from industry to share what it's like to be an engineer.
22		George Washington's Birthday	Our first president was born on this day in 1732. Create an interactive presentation in the program of your choice. Highlight the monuments and major historical sites in Washington, D.C. Research and use maps to complete this project. Start your first slide with the Washington Monument. Place a directional button at the top to go north. Link that button to the White House and embellish your slide with pertinent information. South will lead you the Jefferson Memorial. Where will east and west take you?
23		Curling is Cool Day	Curling is an Olympic sport. Players slide stones on a sheet of ice towards a target of concentric circles. Tabletop curling is also fun. In this shuffleboard style team game, pairs of students slide a unique bottle top towards a target. The target is a 2 by 2 inch square of tape at the end of a table. Players take turns flicking the bottle cap across the table while the second player (known as the sweeper) blows the cap toward the target. The winning cap is the one closest to the middle of the target.

24		National Trading Card Day	Trading cards are collectable cards that have been part of America's history and are traditionally connected to baseball. Cards are usually printed on paperboard and contain an image of a person, place or thing along with a short description or a trivia fact. There are cards for all kinds of subjects. Create your own card for a topic of your choice. For example, famous inventors or presidents of the United States. Using a computer, try out the free Trading Card Creator at: http://www.readwritethink.org/classroom-resources/student-interactives/trading-card-creator-30056.html
25		Quiet Day	Plan a day of quiet activities. Create an eight-page booklet out of two pieces of paper. Write and illustrate your "Kid's Guide to Quiet Day." Write a sentence about each and illustrate your page. Here are a few ideas to get your gears in your head going, quietly of course. Watch a Charlie Chaplin silent movie. Play a game of solitaire. What eight things will you do to celebrate National Quiet Day?
26		Levi Strauss Day	Levi Jeans are truly all-American. First introduced in 1873, the jeans found immortality by coming to represent the American West. They were embraced by young and old alike and became a social phenomenon. What other products are truly made in America? Select one of the following all-American inventions and create a brief history on a presentation slide. Choose from Monopoly®, McDonalds®, Levi® Jeans or Coca Cola®.

27		National Strawberry Day	Strawberries make wonderful jams, jellies and preserves. For this science experiment, discover the effect of lemon juice, water and sugar on the preservation of strawberries. Separately fill ½ cup of sugar, lemon juice and water into three glasses. Place two strawberries into each glass. Seal with plastic wrap and a rubber band. Label the glasses and observe and record what happens daily for seven days. When does discoloration, change of size and/or mold begin to form? Which resulted in edible strawberries and why? Write up your results.
28		International Tongue Twister Day	Find ten tongue twisters and hold a tongue twister contest to see who can read the twister the fastest without making any errors. Here's a famous one to get you started: Peter Piper picked a peck of pickled peppers. A peck of pickled peppers Peter Piper picked. If Peter Piper picked a peck of pickled peppers, where's the peck of pickled peppers Peter Piper picked?
29		Leap Day	Julius Caesar in 45 B.C.E. proposed changing the calendar to accommodate the fact that it takes 365 days, 5 hours, 48 minutes and 45 seconds to complete a trip around the sun. So every four years those extra hours add up to an extra day and an extra three days every 400 years. In 1582, Pope Gregory XIII abolished the Julian calendar and established the Gregorian calendar. Now the discrepancy is only 26 seconds a year and won't add up to a full day for another 3,323 years. How do you tell if it is a Leap Year? Leap Years are years that can be evenly divided by 4 (like 2016, 2020) or can be evenly divided by 400 (like 2000, 2400). Years that can be evenly divided by 100 (like 2000, 2100, etc.) are not. For Leap Year Day, find ten historical events and calculate if that was a leap year. Was the year you were born a leap year?

February Overview

National Freedom Day
Science Lesson: Presidential Graphology
Poetry Lesson: Of Old Sat Freedom on the Heights
by Alfred Lord Tennyson
This day observes the signing of the 13th Amendment by President Lincoln. Student scientists learn about graphology and use their knowledge to analyze presidential personalities. In the poetry lesson students personify "Freedom."

Presidents' Day
Technology Lesson: Presidential Mosaic
Poetry Lesson: from The People, Yes by Carl Sandburg
Presidents' Day is celebrated on the third Monday in February to honor our presidents. In this technology lesson, students find five to ten little-known facts about a president and create a fancy poster using word processing software. In the poetry lesson, students write about issues they believe the president of their choice would or would not support.

Black History
Engineering Lesson: Making Plaster Face Masks
Poetry Lesson We Wear the Mask
by Paul Laurence Dunbar
February is the month that is set aside to remember and celebrate the contributions of African Americans. Students study Dunbar's poem and engineer masks.

Valentine's Day
Math Lesson: Memory-Matching Game
Poetry Lesson: A Red, Red Rose by Robert Burns
Valentine's Day became popular in the United States in the 1800s when Esther Howland began mass-producing cards. Today, millions of people send and receive cards. Student mathematicians work together to create math concentration games using candy kisses. In the poetry lesson, students model a poem written by Burns for a valentine to someone special.

Science Lesson for National Freedom Day: Presidential Graphology

In this lesson, students create personality profiles of selected presidents using the science of graphology, commonly called handwriting analysis. Freedom for all Americans is celebrated on February 1st, commemorating the day that President Lincoln signed the 13th amendment abolishing slavery. Many other presidents also signed documents that expanded the freedom of American citizens. President Woodrow Wilson signed the 19th amendment giving voting rights to women. President Lyndon B. Johnson signed the Voting Rights Act of 1965, which is widely considered to be one of the most important civil rights legislations ever enacted. President Barack Obama signed the bill repealing "don't ask, don't tell" giving gays and lesbians the right to serve openly in the military.

MATERIALS

- Handwriting Analysis and Presidential Signatures Handouts
- Paper and pencil
- Board or chart paper with markers
- Word processing software (optional)
- Projector

PLAN

- Distribute the Handwriting Analysis Handout.
- Discuss each of the most common individual handwriting traits described on the handout (pressure, baseline, size, zones, spacing between letters, spacing between words, and signatures).
- After students have discussed the traits, ask students to study the signature of Abraham Lincoln on the handout and analyze his personality.

DO

- Divide the class into groups of four or five students.
- Distribute the Presidential Signatures Handout to each group.
- Determine a time for the group to complete the following:
    - Group members select three or four interesting presidential signatures to analyze.
    - Students take notes on what the signatures indicate about the personalities of the presidents they chose.
    - Each group selects a member to report the group's findings to the class.
    - Project the signatures on the board and have the reporter for each group share their findings with the class.

EXTENDING THE LESSON

Students research one of the presidents whose signature they analyzed to find out as much as they can about his personality. Students write a comparison between the handwriting analysis and the personality facts they learned through research.

Handwriting Analysis Handout

Graphologists look at many components of writing styles when analyzing handwriting. Use the list below to learn about some of the most common handwriting trait indicators and use them to analyze the handwriting of U.S. Presidents.

PRESSURE

- Heavy – serious, self reliant, bold
- Light – sensitive, honorable, kind

SLANT (right-handed)

- Right slant – assertive, confident, responsive, friendly
- Left slant – loner
- No slant – logical, practical

BASELINE

- Uphill – optimistic, hopeful, energetic
- Downhill – pessimistic
- Even lines – even-tempered, steady

SIZE

- Large – extraverted, outgoing
- Average – practical, realistic, grounded
- Small – a thinker, an academic, analytical

ZONES

Zones are determined by the space in which lower-case letters are written (on the line, above the line, below the line) and whether or not they are emphasized. Examples of emphasized letters are fancy dotted i's, large or fancy looped b's and d's, and long tailed y's.

- Middle zone letters emphasized – (on the line a, c, e, i, m, n, u, and v) - society, reality, and daily life
- Upper zone letters emphasized – (lower case letters that extend above the line – b, d, f, h, k, l, and t) – intellect, spirituality
- Lower zone letters emphasized – (lower case letters that extend below the line – j, g, y, p, q, and z) – money, food, shelter

SPACING BETWEEN LETTERS

- Wide – independent, reserved, loner
- Joined – logical, systematic
- Mixed – artistic, intuitive
- Un-joined – impulsive, sociable

SPACING BETWEEN WORDS

- Wide – needs much personal space and privacy
- Average – feels comfortable in contact with others
- Little or none – needs contact and closeness with others, likes crowds

SIGNATURE

- Legible – confident, comfortable, understandable
- Un-legible – private, hard

Presidential Signatures Handout

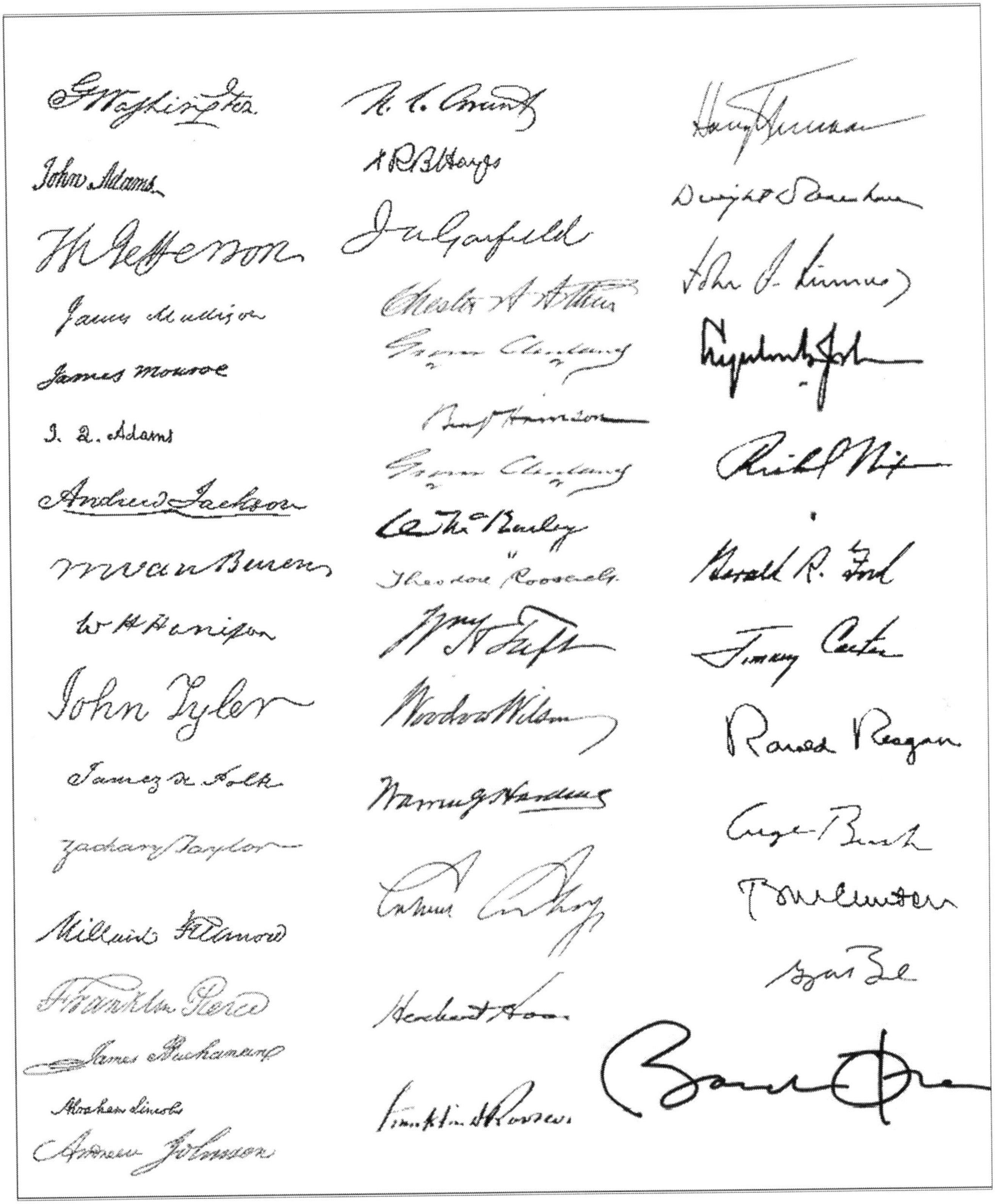

Technology Extension Lesson for National Freedom Day: From Slave to Soldier Civil War Posters

On January 1, 1863 President Abraham Lincoln issued the Emancipation Proclamation. In addition to proclaiming freedom for over three million slaves, the Proclamation also paved the way for black soldiers to enlist in the Union Army. Five months after the Proclamation was signed the War Department of the United States established the United States Colored Troops. Frederick Douglass urged all African Americans to serve. Trading shackles for freedom, Douglas said, "Once let the black man get upon his person the brass letters U.S., let him get an eagle on his button, and a musket on his shoulder and bullets in his pockets, and there is no power on earth which can deny that he has earned the right of citizenship in the United States."

In this lesson students will work with partners to create civil war recruitment posters designed to encourage "colored" men to join the Union Army. An excellent video to show at the beginning of the lesson to spark ideas for the posters is from the Smithsonian Channel at the following website:
http://www.smithsonianchannel.com/videos/from-slave-to-soldier-to-forever-free/23094

PREPARE

Before students begin creating their posters, project the following Civil War recruitment posters from the Library of Congress website:
http://www.librarycompany.org/mcallisterexhibition/section3.htm.

1. Discuss how fonts and graphics are used to focus attention on the messages the poster designers wished to convey.
2. Create a student list of factual and persuasive items to include and write the list on a board or chart.

DO

Working in pairs students use word processing, drawing and/or slide software to create a Union Army recruitment poster.

1. Students use the information from the class list as well as other sources from the Internet to include in the posters.
2. They search the Internet for Civil War recruitment posters to learn how fonts, borders, space and or/graphics are used to draw attention to the messages and create an eye-catching poster of their own.
3. Students print their documents and share them with their classmates.

Poetry Lesson for National Freedom Day: Of Old Sat Freedom on the Heights

In his poem, Alfred Lord Tennyson pictures Freedom as an "old" goddess since the desire for freedom has existed since the beginning of human time. Even though she sits up high with thunder breaking at her feet and stars shaking, she is calm and joyful. With Freedom, comes joy and peace. She steps down from her position near the stars "To mingle with the human race," to become not only a concept but also a reality. She rules over nature "God-like" and rules "King-like" as she "wears the crown." As she stands near us, she will "Make bright our days and light our dreams."

MATERIALS

- Alfred Lord Tennyson Biography and his poem *Of Old Sat Freedom on the Heights*
- Word processing or desktop publishing software or pencil, pens and paper
- Art materials for illustration

PLAN

Read and discuss Tennyson's biography and poem.
Some sample guiding questions include:

- Where are examples of personification?
- Who is "she" and why does Tennyson write "she" is "old"?
- Why does "she" leave her place up high and travel where the people live?
- What does "she" desire?
- Why does Tennyson write "That her fair form may stand and shine?"
- What does Tennyson say "Freedom" will do?

DO

Getting Ready to Write

During a class discussion use some of the questions below:

- What human features does your "Freedom" have?
- Where would your "Freedom" live?
- What does your "Freedom" look like?
- What does he or she say to you?
- What would your "Freedom" tell you about himself or herself?
- What would your "Freedom" tell you about what was accomplished?
- What would "Freedom" still like to accomplish?
- What makes "Freedom" happy and sad?
- What else do you think "Freedom" would say to you?

Writing the Poem

- Using personification, students write poems about Freedom. Suggest they begin their poem describing where Freedom lives.
- Have students complete their poems by continuing their conversations with Freedom.
- Have students create a poetic look on the page rather than that of an essay.

Editing and Publishing

- Students read and edit poems with partners discussing each other's use of personification.
- Students write their poems in a poetry book or enter them in a word processing program and illustrate their final masterpiece by drawing a picture.

Poet for National Freedom Day
Alfred Lord Tennyson Biography
August 6, 1809 - October 6, 1892

Alfred Lord Tennyson is considered to be the greatest of the Victorian poets and was the most popular English poet of his time. Although Tennyson's father was a reverend, he didn't grow up in a peaceful environment. He had eleven brothers and sisters. His father was an alcoholic. One sibling was emotionally disturbed and another was addicted to drugs. There was a lot of arguing in his home between his father and one of his brothers.

Tennyson began to write poetry before he was ten years old. His father helped Alfred by tutoring him in classical and modern languages to prepare him for college. By the time he was 18, he had published his first volume. When he began his studies at Cambridge University, his success as a poet made him very popular with a group of gifted students who encouraged him to devote his life to poetry. The friendships he formed at Cambridge gave him confidence to continue his work as a poet.

Although Tennyson did not have a happy childhood, he enjoyed his adult life. He got married and had a family. His earnings from poetry enabled him to buy a house in the country and to enjoy the kind of solitude he liked. He was a true character with his cloak and big hat. His powerful voice captured his listeners. In addition to being a poet, Tennyson was a wise man whose ideas on politics and world affairs represented the voice of his nation. Queen Victoria recognized him with the title of poet laureate.

Tennyson had the power of creating scenery and states of feeling through his writing. He examined many religious issues that bewildered both his generation and future generations.

Of Old Sat Freedom on the Heights
by Alfred Lord Tennyson

Of old sat Freedom on the heights,
The thunders breaking at her feet:
Above her shook the starry lights:
She heard the torrents meet.
There in her place she did rejoice,
Self-gather'd in her prophet-mind,
But fragments of her mighty voice
Came rolling on the wind.
Then stept she down thro' town and field
To mingle with the human race,
And part by part to men reveal'd
The fulness of her face--

Grave mother of majestic works,
From her isle-altar gazing down,
Who, God-like, grasps the triple forks,
And, King-like, wears the crown:

Her open eyes desire the truth.
The wisdom of a thousand years
Is in them. May perpetual youth
Keep dry their light from tears;

That her fair form may stand and shine,
Make bright our days and light our dreams,
Turning to scorn with lips divine
The falsehood of extremes!

Music Lesson for National Freedom Day: The Power of Music

National Freedom Day was enacted to celebrate Abraham Lincoln's signing of the 13th Amendment giving all Americans freedom. Richard Robert Wright Sr., a former slave, felt the need for people to remember this date and the importance of freedom. He began a movement to make the signing a national holiday. February 1st was chosen to celebrate the holiday since that was the date that President Lincoln signed the 13th Amendment. Expressing freedom through music has a long history in our country. Woody Guthrie, was a songwriter who wrote "This Land Is Your Land" a song that would become an unofficial national anthem sung in classrooms around the nation. Students are introduced to his patriotic song in which he expresses his ideas of freedom. Students analyze the beat and the lyrics of the song and create their own song imitating the same beat and as they reflect on their own ideas of freedom.

MATERIALS

Paper, pens, pencils
YouTube recording of "This Land is Your Land" –
https://www.youtube.com/watch?v=wxiMrvDbq3s
"This Land is Your Land" song lyrics printed

Play song and then discuss the following questions:

- How does Guthrie define the freedom that our country offers?
- How do you experience freedom is your life?

Students do the following:

- Listen to the music and lyrics of Woody Guthrie's "This Land is Your Land."
- Clap the following words to find how many beats are in each word.
  California, New York Island, Redwood forest, Gulf stream waters
- How many beats did they discover?
- Begin their lyrics by copying the first line of the chorus, "This land is your land, this land is my land."
- In the second and third lines replace the words they have clapped with words of their own mimicking the same beat.
  For example: *From my best friend Joey and my neighbor Linda,*
  From the tall skyscrapers to the green baseball field
- End their song lyrics by copying the last line, "This land was made for you and me."

Students perform their lyrics in a small group and with the class:

- Divide class into five or six groups
- Group members sing the first line of the song in unison and each group member adds their own original second and third lines, followed by the last line of the song sung together.
- After practicing their new original songs, each group performs for the class.

This Land Is Your Land

Words and music by Woody Guthrie

These are well-known lyrics, however the song has many versions and incarnations.

Chorus:
This land is your land, this land is my land
From California, to the New York Island
From the Redwood forest, to the Gulf stream waters
This land was made for you and me

Stanza:
As I was walking a ribbon of highway
I saw above me an endless skyway
I saw below me a golden valley
This land was made for you and me

Chorus

Stanza:
I've roamed and rambled and I've followed my footsteps
To the sparkling sands of her diamond deserts
And all around me a voice was sounding
This land was made for you and me

Chorus

Stanza:
The sun comes shining as I was strolling
The wheat fields waving and the dust clouds rolling
The fog was lifting a voice come chanting
This land was made for you and me

Technology Lesson for President's Day: Little-Known Presidential Facts Mosaic

In this project, students use the Internet to find at least five little-known facts about a United States president. After opening a new blank page in a word processing program, students first place a picture of that president on the page and then use text in a creative way to produce a mosaic of little-known facts. The final works of art can be mounted on red, white or blue construction paper and displayed on a President's Day bulletin board.

MATERIALS

- Computer, word processing software and Internet access
- Red, white and blue art paper
- Glue, tape, other mounting materials
- Paper and pencils

PLAN

- Display a list of United States presidents on a chart or bulletin board.
- Have students share information they know about the presidents on the list.
- Students pick a president and find from five to ten interesting little-known facts.

DO

- Students select a president to research.
- They find five to ten little-known facts about the president they have chosen through an Internet search and write a sentence for each fact on a sheet of paper.
- Students search the Internet for an image of the president selected and save.
- They open a word processing document and paste the image into the document on the center of the page.
- Students type the title of the page "Little-Known Facts About [the president selected]."
- Next, they type five to ten sentences into the document.
- They highlight each of the sentences, one at a time, and use font options, colors, sizes and rotating features to create a mosaic out of their sentences.
- Students save and print their documents and share them with their classmates in an oral presentation, on the bulletin board or in a class book.

George Washington was an excellent dancer

Science Extension Lesson for President's Day: Lincoln Pennies – Buoyancy, Density and Displacement

In this lesson, student STEM scientists discover and discuss how an object's buoyancy and density determines whether it will sink in water. They also observe the distance an object sinks due to how much water it displaces. After predicting and discovering whether several objects sink or float, students work in groups to build tin foil boats. Groups enter their boats into a Lincoln Penny Competition. The winning boat is the one that holds the most Lincoln pennies without sinking or tipping.

MATERIALS

- Solid objects: wood blocks, apples, balloons, paper clips, pennies, car keys, stapler and more
- Clay
- Baby bathtub or small plastic swimming pool
- Tin foil
- Aluminum trays
- Water
- Pennies
- Abraham Lincoln Buoyancy Worksheet

Do the following to develop an understanding of buoyancy, density and displacement.

1. Fill a baby bathtub or a very small children's swimming pool with water.
2. Give two students a small piece of clay. The first student forms the clay into a small ball and the second shapes the clay into a shallow dish. Students guess whether the bowl and the ball will sink or float and state their reasons.
3. Both students put both clay structures into the water. They observe that the ball sinks and the bowl floats.
4. Discuss how and why buoyancy (the resistance of water pushing against the object) keeps the bowl afloat.
    a. The bowl-shaped clay structure floats because the water it displaces moves out of the way.
    b. The ball-shaped clay structure sinks because it takes up less space in the water. The force of gravity overtakes the force of the water.
5. All boats have a maximum load they can carry without becoming too heavy to float.
6. Give a third student a piece of clay equal in size to the first two and shape the clay into a boat. Place the boat into the water. Have student volunteers pick solid objects to place in the boat, one at a time. Before each new object is placed in the boat, have students predict whether the boat will float or sink.
7. Students discuss how all boats especially those carrying cargo have a limit on the amount of cargo they can hold before sinking.
8. Divide students into small groups and give each group papers and pencils, a few sheets of aluminum foil and a roll of pennies and have them complete the Abraham Lincoln Buoyancy Worksheet.

Abraham Lincoln Buoyancy Worksheet

Draw a picture of your boat design.

Fold a sheet of tin foil into the shape you designed. Fill the aluminum tray with water and place the boat in the water. Describe its buoyancy.

Take turns placing pennies one at a time in the cargo area of your boat. How many pennies can it hold before it sinks?

Describe ways you can design your boat to increase its cargo hold.

Redesign your boat and enter it into the class Lincoln Penny Competition. How did your boat do?

What was the shape of the ship that remained buoyant with the most pennies?

What would you do differently next time?

Poetry Lesson for President's Day
Excerpt from The People, Yes

This excerpt is from a 300 page book-length poem *The People, Yes*. Carl Sandburg writes about Lincoln and Lincoln's understanding of the positive and negative aspects of a democracy. He valued these contradictions and said "Yes to the paradoxes of democracy."

MATERIALS

- Carl Sandburg Biography and excerpt from *The People, Yes*
- Word processing or desktop publishing software or pencils, pens and paper
- Board or chart and marker

PLAN

Read and discuss Carl Sandburg's biography and poem. Some sample guiding questions include:

- What are some of the paradoxes of democracy in our country?
- In the poem, President Lincoln says, "Yes to the hopes of government." To what else does he say "yes?"
- President Lincoln says, "No to the constitution when a hindrance." To what else does he say "no?"

DO

Getting Ready to Write

During a class discussion, ask students the following questions. Write their responses on a board or chart.

- To which president will they write?
- What issues would they like to discuss with the president they select?

Writing the Poem

- Students title their poem "To (the president of their choice)."
- Suggest that their first line be the name of the president they have selected followed by a question mark.
- Continue their poem telling to what issues they think their president would say "yes" and to what issues they think their president would say "no."
- Students can make their poem more interesting mixing "yes" and "no" lines.

Editing and Publishing

- Students read and edit poems with partners.
- Students read their poems as if they are questioning the president of their choice.

Poet for President's Day
Carl Sandburg Biography
January 6, 1878 - July 22, 1967

Carl Sandburg was born in Illinois. When he was thirteen, he left school and went to work. Initially, he did not have a formal education, but his many jobs gave him much life experience. Sandburg is known as the Poet of the Industrial Revolution. He worked in a theater, barbershop, in a brickyard, as a dishwasher in hotels and as a harvest hand in the wheat fields. These jobs and the people he met through them became the subject matter of his poetry.

In 1898 when war with Spain was declared, Sandburg enlisted into the United States Army. Afterwards, he went to college and became interested in literature. He left college without a degree and traveled the country riding the railroads. Eventually, he became a journalist.

While he worked as a newspaperman, he struggled to keep writing poetry. Sandburg was unknown in the literary world until he was thirty-six years old. A group of his poems finally appeared in a famous poetry journal. A year later, his first book of poems was published. Those in the literary world thought he should pay more attention to the craft of writing. But the reading public appreciated his subjects and his honest words. In his lifetime he won three Pulitzer prizes. Two of them were for his poetry and a third for a biography he wrote about Abraham Lincoln. In 1964 he received the Presidential Medal of Freedom from President Lyndon B. Johnson.

Excerpt from The People, Yes
by Carl Sandburg

The entire poem is available online. You can search online for it or you can go to the following website and find the poem. It is ready to print and copy.

http://www.poetryfoundation.org/poem/182329

In one portion of his 300 hundred-page poem, Carl Sandburg writes about Abraham Lincoln's views on both the positive and negative aspects of a democratic form of government. Lincoln says "Yes to the hopes of government," "Yes to the Constitution when a help," and "No to the Constitution when a hindrance."

Lincoln saw what was good for the country. He didn't try to have laws passed to harm the people of his land, but to make his land a place where freedom is the right of all people. In the poem, Sandburg quotes Lincoln:

"I have not willingly planted a thorn
in any man's bosom."
I shall do nothing through malice: what
I deal with is too vast for malice."

Art Lesson for President's Day: Presidential Mosaics

Mosaics have been used for over 4,000 years beginning with the ancient Greeks. Romans used mosaic tiles to provide durable walking spaces. They put cement over dirt floors and laid stone chips on top. This made their floors cool and easy to clean. Beautiful and colorful mosaics were used as art forms in baths, villas and temples. This art form was later introduced to America by Italian immigrants. There are a great assortment of materials used for mosaics including pebbles, seashells, precious stones, colored glass, wood and paper. In this extension lesson to celebrate Presidents' Day, students will use an assortment of different papers to make mosaics in the form of a president's portrait.

MATERIALS

- Construction paper
- Assortment of paper – magazines, newspapers, colored paper
- Pencils
- Glue
- Scissors

Students do the following:

1. Find a president of their choice either on the Internet or a book. A good idea is to search for a coloring book portrait.
2. Put the portrait near the piece of paper and copy it onto construction paper.
3. Cut pieces of paper into "tiles" in the shape of squares, diamonds, and triangles.
4. Fill in the design by gluing the tiles to the paper.
5. Keep a small amount of space between the tiles so that it looks like grout.
6. Place and paste the cut out shapes. Press down so that it lies flat.
7. Place, glue, press each cut out shape inside the sketched lines.

Engineering Lesson for Black History Month: We Make the Mask

In this lesson, students make plaster bandage masks that capture the shapes and forms of their faces. They also paint and decorate their masks. This is a messy activity. Planning ahead is critical to making this experience a success.

MATERIALS

- Plastic garbage bags to cover hair and clothing.
- Butcher paper or plastic drop clothes to cover work areas
- Plaster bandages cut into 1"x 4" strips. You will need approximately 5 pounds available at an art or craft supply store
- Petroleum jelly, small dishes of water, scissors, facial soap, paper towels, tempera paint and felt markers
- Water at room temperature
- Mask decorating materials (paint, markers, buttons, yarn, sequins, feathers, felt, etc.)

Lila and Clara - 10th grade

PLAN

- Create a list of famous African American barrier breakers who paved the way for future generations including: Thurgood Marshall, Phillis Wheatley, Jackie Robinson, Rosa Parks, Barack Obama and Althea Gibson.
- Display and discuss the Sidney Poitier quote:

  > "So I had to be careful. I recognized the responsibility that, whether I liked it or not, I had to accept whatever the obligation was. That was to behave in a manner, to carry myself in such a professional way, as if there ever is a reflection, it's a positive."
- Discuss why and how the African Americans listed may have had to "wear a mask" to present acceptable expressions and behaviors in order to remove barriers for future generations.
- Students create a base mask of their faces that will be painted and decorated.
- Pair up students. One will be the "maker" who will create the mask and the other the "model" for the mask. They will reverse roles after the first mask is complete.
- This is a messy activity. The student models should cover themselves up with a smock or cut a hole for their head in a garbage bag and slip it on over their clothing. They also need to pull their hair away from their foreheads and cover their hair with a plastic bag. The workspace should also be covered.
- Place a bowl of water and the pre-cut plaster bandages near each pair of students.

DO

- Each pair decides who will be the first maker and the first model.
- The maker applies a thin coat of petroleum jelly to the skin of the model's face next to the hairline and on the eyebrows.
- With the model keeping his/her head back, the maker builds the mask one bandage at a time by dipping it individually into the water dish and placing it gently on the face.
- As the bandages are wrapped, they are overlapped. Each new strip is patted down and smoothed so it is flush against the skin.
- Apply extra bandages to reinforce the strength of the mask and have the maker check for any uncovered skin and cover it.
- Leave the eyes and nostrils uncovered.
- After about five minutes and if the mask feels dry to the touch, the model should slowly moves his/her face to loosen the mask while the maker pries at the edges with spread fingertips.
- When the mask is removed, the maker should build up weak areas with additional plaster bandages.
- After wiping thoroughly with dry paper towels, the model washes with soap and water to clean off.
- Maker and model reverse roles and repeat the process.
- When the masks have thoroughly hardened, students decorate them.

EXTENSIONS

- Display each mask with the poem written by the student.
- Photograph the masks and record the poems.
- Combine the two to make a digitized slide show.
- Place the shows on a CD, upload to a website or distribute to go home via a flash drive.

Math Extension for Black History Month: Mancala

During Black History Month students learn to play Mancala, a game of counting and strategy that originated in ancient Africa. The game is easily learned but requires a great deal of strategy to win. After creating the game boards, the class pairs up and proceeds to play.

MATERIALS NEEDED FOR EACH GAME BOARD

Egg cartons
Two small bowls or boxes
Playing pieces – 48 each of beans, pebbles, marbles, coins, jelly beans or other small objects
Paint and paintbrushes (optional)

MAKING THE GAME BOARDS AND SETTING UP THE GAME

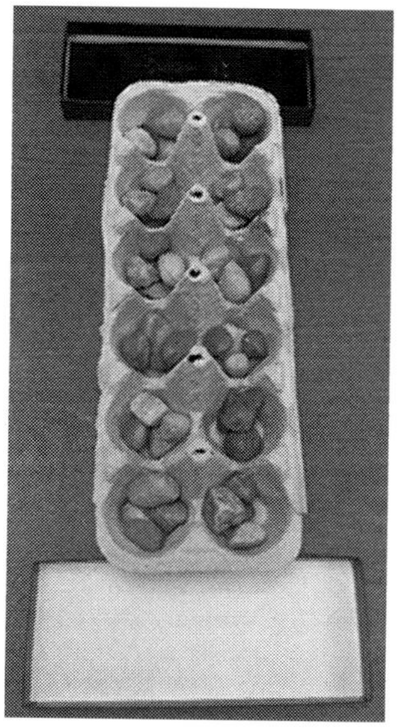

The Mancala game board has two rows of six pockets known as pits. Students use an empty egg carton to make a game board by following the directions below:

1. Remove the top and use the bottom half with 12 pockets. You may paint the egg carton.
2. Each player puts a small bowl or box to one side of the Mancala board. These are known as the stores.
3. Distribute the 48 playing pieces evenly among the 12 pits (4 per pit).

PLAYING MANCALA

The game Mancala is played all over the world and students who have played the game may have played in a slightly modified way. Demonstrate how to play the game using the rules below. We suggest watching a video of game play on YouTube.

1. One player picks up all of the pieces in any of the pits on his side to begin.
2. Moving counter-clockwise, the player deposits one of the stones in each pit until the stones run out.
3. When the player runs into his/her own store, the player places one piece in it.
4. If the player runs into the opponent's store, he/she skips it.
5. The player gets a free turn if the last piece dropped is in the player's store.
6. If the last piece dropped is in an empty pit on the player's side, the player captures that piece and any pieces in the pit directly opposite. All captured pieces are placed into the player's store.
7. A turn is defined as depositing 4 stones and any implications as stated above. When the first player's turn is completed, the second player begins.
8. The game ends when all six pits on one side of the board are empty.
9. The player who still has pieces on his/her side of the board when the game ends captures all of those pieces.
10. The player who has the most pieces in his/her store is the winner.

In the game of Mancala, the person who goes first has an advantage. If possible, have the players repeat the game reversing playing order. Students can continue to hone their Mancala strategies online. Some websites geared for student math play are: http://www.coolmath-games.com/0-mancala and http://www.mathplayground.com/mancala.html.

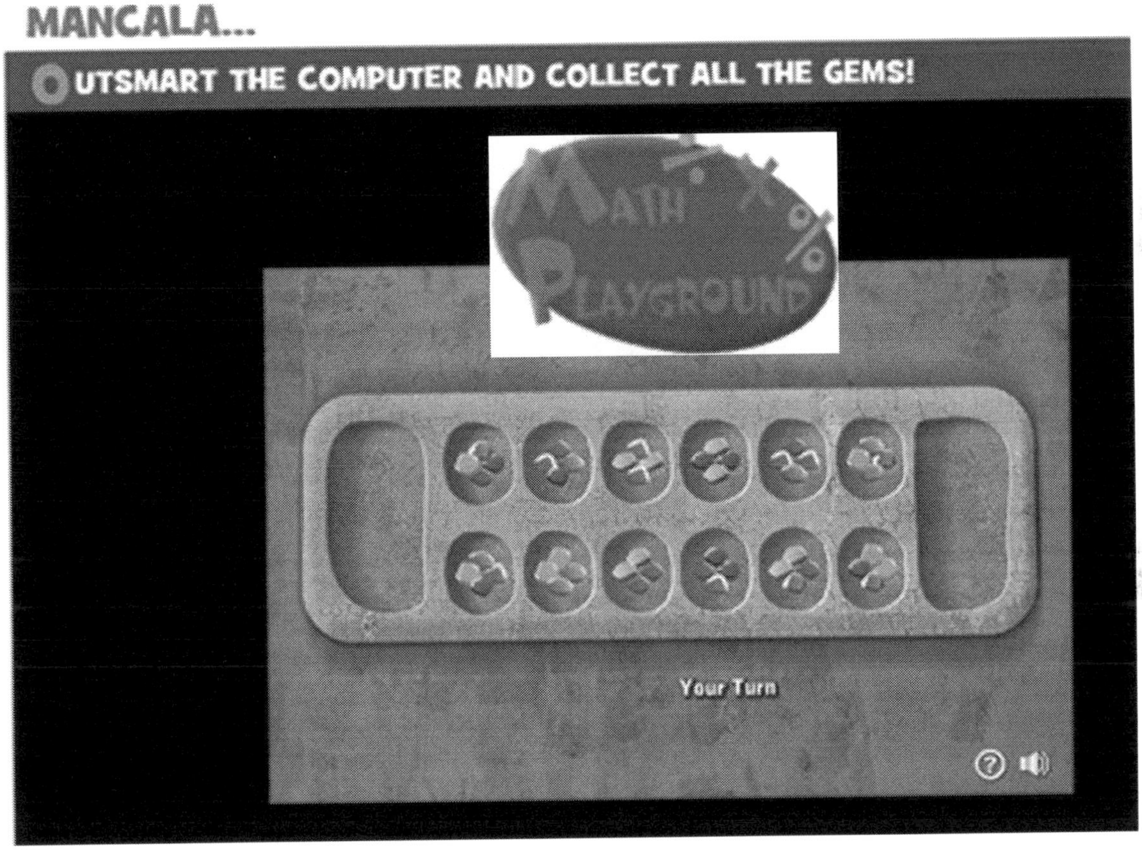

Poetry Lesson for Black History Month: We Wear the Mask

In his poem *We Wear the Mask*, Paul Laurence Dunbar speaks to African Americans who covered their anguish and agony by wearing a "mask that grins and lies." The mask is an extended metaphor used to show the need to hide "their torn and bleeding hearts." The mask was the armor they used to hide their vulnerability from the prejudice they faced.

MATERIALS

- Paul Laurence Dunbar Biography and his poem *We Wear the Mask*
- Word processing or desktop publishing software or pencil, pens and paper
- Construction paper
- Digital camera

PLAN

Discuss Dunbar's biography and poem asking the following questions:

- Why and where does Dunbar use the mask as a metaphor?
- Why does Dunbar use "we" throughout the poem? Who does the word "we" represent?
- Ask students why it was necessary to wear a mask?

DO

Getting Ready to Write

During a brainstorming session, ask students the following questions. As the class gives their responses, encourage discussion.

- What experiences have you had where you wear a mask?
- In what ways do you or your friends mask your true feelings?
- What experiences have your friends had when they wear a mask?
- Were your friends able to mask their feelings?

Writing the Poem

- Students title their poems "I Wear a Mask."
- Suggest they start the body of their poem with, "I wear a mask that" and continue with what their mask does.
  For example: *I wear a mask that smiles and laughs.*
- Students continue the poem describing different experiences that happened that made them wear the mask.
  For example: *when my friends laughed at my mistake* or *when someone told me my hair was too curly*
- They include descriptions of where they feel safe to take off their masks
  For example: *in their bedroom, in front of their mom, etc.*
- They also include what they do when their masks are off. For example, *cry into their pillow, etc.*

Editing and Publishing

- Students read and edit poems with partners.
- Students take a picture of themselves using the face they use when their mask is on and when their mask is off.
- Students mount their poems with photos on construction paper.
- The finished products are displayed around the room.

Poet for Black History Month
Paul Laurence Dunbar Biography
June 27, 1872 - February 9, 1906

Paul Laurence Dunbar was born in Dayton, Ohio. Both his mother and father had been slaves. His father escaped from slavery and served as a soldier in the Civil War. His mother was a freed slave. Although his family was poor, his mother provided him with a rich education filled with her love of storytelling and songs. She even learned to read to help him with his schooling.

By the time he entered school at age six, he was reading and writing poetry. In school, he was part of the debate team, president of the literary society and editor of the school paper. He was a very successful student.

Dunbar was the first African-American poet to achieve fame as a writer. In much of his poems, short stories and novels, he wrote about the problems that faced his race. He was versatile and wrote not only in standard English but also in dialect. Dunbar's work is known for its colorful language and conversational tone.

After his first book of poetry was published, both writers and critics saw his great talent. His popularity grew. When his second book of poetry was published, he was asked to do a reading in London. At this point of Dunbar's career and at the age of 25, he had achieved fame both nationally and internationally. President Theodore Roosevelt honored him with a ceremonial sword.

Dunbar died at the young age of 33 from tuberculosis. He was internationally respected and his renowned work will never be forgotten. In 1975, a 10-cent postage stamp was issued in his honor.

We Wear the Mask
By Paul Laurence Dunbar

We wear the mask that grins and lies,
It hides our cheeks and shades our eyes,
This debt we pay to human guile;
With torn and bleeding hearts we smile,
And mouth with myriad subtleties.

Why should the world be over-wise,
In counting all our tears and sighs?
Nay, let them only see us, while
We wear the mask.

We smile, but, O great Christ, our cries
To thee from tortured souls arise.
We sing, but oh the clay is vile
Beneath our feet, and long the mile;
But let the world dream otherwise,
We wear the mask.

The mask laughs as it tells lies
Debby – 6th grade

Art Lesson for Black History Month: We Draw the Mask

Masks, a well-known art form of Africa, are greatly admired. For centuries, African people used masks in ceremonies and rituals. Lois Mallou Jones gave new life to the African mask. In this lesson, students draw masks using her work as a model

MATERIALS

- Drawing pencils, erasers, felt tip pen
- Letter size black construction paper
- Black construction paper
- Brightly colored construction paper for mounting
- White pencil and other colored pencils
- Interact capable device
- Lois Mailou Jones Biography

Students do the following:

1. Students read the biography of Lois Mailou Jones.
2. Search the Internet for images of her masks.
3. Select favorite masks to use as models for their mask drawings.
4. Sketch their interpretation of the painting with a white pencil.
5. Draw the shape of the face.
6. Draw the facial features with closed shapes. For example, triangular eyes, crescent-shaped eyebrows, and circular checks.
7. Use colored pencils to enhance and fill in the face. For a brighter effect, fill first with a white pencil and color over with another color.
8. Draw the background using her design patterns for inspiration.
9. Mount the drawing on brightly colored construction paper.
10. Share your artwork with the class.

EXTENSION

- Students photograph their finished mask and place it in a Black History Month Slideshow.
- Create a Black History Month display. Mount the pictures and student poems side by side for maximum impact.

Lois Mailou Jones Biography
November 13, 1905 - June 9, 1998

Lois Mailou Jones was an African American artist. She began her lifelong career of painting at a young age. Jones was encouraged by her parents who supplied her with crayons, paper and pencils. She is quoted as saying "As a child I was always drawing. I loved color." In the 1930s and 1940s, her paintings became internationally famous which was an unheard of achievement for an African American woman. In 1937, she painted "Les Fetiches," one of her most famous mask paintings.

Jones encountered much prejudice in the United States. It was not until she went to France in the 1930s that she felt like a free individual. France gave her a sense of security and also knowledge that she was a talented artist. The subjects of her paintings were Parisian people and the landscapes she observed in France. They were done in the impressionist style of art with huge palette knives on large canvasses.

After leaving France, she returned to the United States and her Paris paintings achieved the fame she deserved. Upon a friend's influence she began to paint black subjects. After marrying, she spent time in Haiti. Her style and colors changed. Her paintings took on the bright colors of people in a Haitian marketplace.

For many years, masks fascinated her. Her later masks were influenced by her visits to African museums where she studied and made sketches of the African designs to use in her paintings.

Mathematics Lesson for Valentine's Day: Math Memory Matching Game with Candy Kisses

In this delicious Valentine themed lesson, students work in groups to create and play math memory matching games. They build the games by writing paired problems and solutions on the bottom of candy kisses.

MATERIALS

- Candy kisses (30 per group)
- Round 3/4 inch self-sticking labels (30 per group)
- Black fine-tipped markers (several per group)
- Chart paper or board

PLAN

- During a class discussion, have students suggest paired math problems and solutions for math concepts they are learning.
- Write their suggestions on a board or chart. For example:
  - 3 x 8 = 24 (multiplication)
  - 1/4 + 1/4 = 1/2 (addition of equivalent fractions)
  - 2 pints = 1 quart (measurement)
- After demonstrating how to create matched problems with the Hershey's Kisses and the self-sticking labels, divide the class into small groups to create memory matching games with candy kisses.
- Distribute candy kisses, self-sticking labels and felt tipped pens to each group.

DO

- Students work together to create and write fifteen math problems and their solutions on pairs of round labels.
- Place the labels on the bottom of the candy kisses.
- Mix the kisses and lay out a table.
- Taking turns, turn over two kisses at a time.
- When they match a problem with its solution, they keep the kisses.
- The person who has the most kisses wins.
- If time permits, have students lay their kisses back on the table and change places with another group.
- Continue game play with the new math problems.
- After the last time the game is played, students divide and eat the Hershey's Kisses.

Noa – 4th grade

Engineering Extension Lesson: Food Engineers

Food engineers are a group of professionals who create, test and bring food to market. Their creations are found on the shelves of markets, fast-food operations and even on space shuttles. In this lesson, students become food engineers, working in groups to create party mixes for Valentine's Day. They select from a group of available food items to create a product that combines compatible flavors, textures, sweetness, saltiness, crunchiness and is also a delight to the eyes. As a final design project, students create a product tag that will seal their party mix. Students complete the project near Valentine's Day and take home one of the completed mixes.

MATERIALS

- Party mix ingredients
- Construction paper
- Double-sided tape
- Self-sealing sandwich size clear plastic bags
- Decorative Valentine's Day stickers
- Latex gloves

PLAN

We are a nation of snackers. Ninety-four per cent of adults say they snack at least once a day according to FoodEngineeringmag.com. Most people crave snacks that are salty, sweet, colorful and crunchy. Students engineer a Valentine's Day Party Mix that tastes good but is also eye-appealing. Students work in small groups as a team to create and package their product.

- Tell students they are doing work as food engineers. Explain that food engineers play an important role in every major area of production each time a new food product is brought to market.
- The new food product will meet specific design criteria. It will be a combination of salty, sweet and crunchy ingredients that will fit into a self-sealing sandwich bag. During a class discussion, make a list of products that would meet these criteria. Possible items include:
  - Mini pretzels
  - A variety of cereals – Strawberry Burst Cheerios, Cinnamon Life, Chocolate Chex, Cap'n Crunch, Fruit Loops
  - Chocolate Teddy Grahams
  - Small dried fruit such as cherries and cranberries
  - Yogurt covered raisins and pretzels
  - Nuts (if there are no food allergies to worry about)
  - M&Ms in Valentine's Day colors (note even plain M&Ms may contain peanuts)
  - Valentine Candy Corn
  - Pink mini marshmallows
  - Frosted animal cookies
  - Popcorn
- Students engineer snacks from the list they create. Fill-in as with other ingredients necessary so that there is a great variety.

DO

- Divide the class into food engineering groups.
- Have students wash their hands and put on latex gloves before handling food items.
- Have the groups select up to six food items for their Valentine assortment. Remind them they need a minimum of one sweet, one crunchy, one salty and one colorful ingredient.
- Have each member take one each of the items selected and do the following:
  - Evaluate how the items look when grouped together.
  - Taste them as a combined assortment to see how the flavors blend.
  - Determine whether they are satisfied that all items in the assortment work well together.
  - Have them make substitutions until they feel they have the best possible assortment.
- Have students arrange the completed assortment in the baggie to create one prototype. Tell students this is an important step in the development of the product, because the way the arrangement looks determines the eye appeal.
- Have students rearrange the mix until they think it looks best.
- When the final prototype is agreed upon, have each group member fill a bag with the party mix using the prototype as a guide.
- To complete the product, have group members create and attach tent labels for the top of their sandwich bags as follows:
  - Cut 6.5" x 4" rectangles from card stock.
  - Fold the rectangles in half so that each half measures 6.5" x 2".
  - Create a prototype with a Valentine's Day message on each side.
  - Copy the prototype to create a label for each party mix created.
  - Place double-sided tape on the inside of the label and attach the label to the sandwich bag.
- Show off your product to the class and place the finished products on a display table.
- When all products have been presented, each student selects a party mix from the table to eat and enjoy.

Logan – 3rd grade

Poetry Lesson for Valentine's Day: A Red, Red Rose

There couldn't be a more perfect poem for Valentine's Day than Robert Burn's *A Red, Red Rose.* With the use of similes, Burns compares his "Luve" to the beauty of a rose, "O my Luve is like a red, red rose." He pledges to love her forever "Till a' the seas gang dry."

MATERIALS

- Robert Burns Biography and his poem *A Red, Red Rose*
- Word processing or desktop publishing software or pencil, pens and paper
- Red construction paper doilies, heart stickers, candy hearts, and more

PLAN

- Read and discuss Robert Burns biography and poem.
- Discuss the poem with the following questions:
  - Where in the poem does Burns write in a Scottish dialect?
  - Where does he use similes?
  - How do you know he will love his "luve" forever?

DO

Getting Ready to Write

- Students write a Valentine to an important person in their life.
  For example: *their mother, father, grandparent, aunt or uncle.*
- Ask the following questions and list a few responses on the board to stimulate ideas.
  - To what beautiful object would you compare this person?
  - What things in the universe will last forever?
  - What things will never happen?

Writing the Poem

- Students title their poems to their chosen person.
- Students follow the steps below to write their poems:
  1. Have them use at least two similes in the first stanza comparing that person to something beautiful, warm or comforting.
  2. In the second stanza, have students tell their person they will love them forever using at least two examples of things that will never end or never happen.

Editing and Publishing

Print or handwrite completed poems on red paper and decorate them using some of the materials listed above to give an original touch to their valentine poems.

Poet for Valentine's Day
Robert Burns Biography
January 25, 1759 - July 21, 1796

Robert Burns, poet, writer and songwriter was born on January 25, 1759 in an ancient village on the west coast of Scotland. Although his parents were poor farmers, it was important to them that their son received a good education, which he began at the age of six.

Because of his family's poor financial condition, Burns was forced to work as a farm laborer. His first love, Nelly Kirkpatrick, encouraged him to write poetry. He wrote regularly and passionately. By the time he was 27, his poems, most of which written in the Scottish dialect, had become famous throughout his country.

He died at 37 and was buried with full civil and military honors. Many of his songs and poems have become more famous after his death, gaining international popularity. He is known as the national poet of Scotland. He has influenced much of Scottish literature.

A Red, Red Rose
by Robert Burns

O my Luve is like a red, red rose
That's newly sprung in June;
O my Luve is like the melody
That's sweetly played in tune.

So fair art thou, my bonnie lass,
So deep in luve am I;
And I will luve thee still, my dear,
Till a' the seas gang dry.

Till a' the seas gang dry, my dear,
And the rocks melt wi' the sun;
I will luv thee still, my dear,
While the sands o' life shall run.

And fare thee weel, my only luve!
And fare thee weel awhile!
And I will come again, my luve,
Though it were ten thousand mile.

Additional Poetry Lesson for Valentine's Day: Sonnet 18

William Shakespeare's *Sonnet 18* is considered to be his most famous love sonnet. An English sonnet is a poem of fourteen lines with ten syllables per line and follows a rhyming scheme. Shakespeare begins with a question addressed to his love comparing her to a summer's day: "Shall I compare thee to a summer's day?" He continues with this comparison that differentiates his love from a summer's day. He explains that his love is lovelier, milder and will endure longer than the summer: "Thy eternal summer shall not fade." Summer is short and will fade whereas his love will last eternally through human memory. Shakespeare writes that as long as there is breath in men, his poetry will endure. In this lesson, students compare their love to a day in their favorite season.

MATERIALS

- William Shakespeare Biography and his poem *Sonnet 18*
- Word Processing or desktop publishing software or pencil, pens and paper
- Red construction paper, doilies, heart stickers, candy hearts and more

PLAN

- Read and discuss William Shakespeare's biography and poem.
- Discuss the poem using the following questions:
    - How does Shakespeare compare summer to his love?
    - What does his love have that summer does not have?
    - How will his love last forever?

DO

Getting Ready to Write

- Each student writes a Valentine to an important person in his or her life:
  For example: *mother, father, grandparent, aunt or uncle.*
- Discuss the following:
    - To what season and to what part of a day would you compare this person?
      For example: *a fall day, a summer night, a spring afternoon, a winter morning*
    - Compare the qualities of the person to a day or a part of the day.
      For example: *you are more dependable than the changing weather of a spring afternoon*
    - Why will your favorite person endure longer than the season?
      For example: *my thoughts of you will stay with me longer than the spring showers*

Writing the Poem

- Suggest students title their poem, "To My Valentine."
- Begin poems with "Shall I compare you to a [day or a part of a day in their favorite season]?
  For example: *a winter morning, a summer day, a spring afternoon, a fall evening*
- Continue the poem comparing the qualities of the person they love with the part of the day they choose.
  For example: *You are warmer and more comforting than the biting cold of a winter morning; You are milder than the blazing sun of a summer's day; You are less chilling than the cooler night of a fall evening*

- Continue writing four more comparisons.
- End the poem describing how the person will endure longer than the season.
  For example: *In my heart you will endure longer than the winter morning; My memory of you will last longer than the heat of summer; You will warm my soul longer than the cool evening of fall.*

Editing and Publishing

Print or handwrite completed poems and mount on red construction paper hearts and doilies. Embellish with other art materials.

Shall I compare you to the trees of autumn?
Your hair is more golden as it flows with the wind
With roots more grounded providing everlasting strength

Mia - 7th grade

Poet for Valentine's Day
William Shakespeare Biography
April 23, 1564 - April 23, 1616

William Shakespeare was born in Stratford-upon-Avon, a town in south Warwickshire, England. His father was a glove maker and tradesman. Shakespeare's mother was the daughter of a farmer. William had seven siblings.

There is much speculation about his life because there are few known facts. He probably attended a grammar school in his town where he would have learned Greek, Latin, mythology, ancient history and other subjects included in a classical education.

His father was in financial debt and therefore Shakespeare did not attend a university. At eighteen, he married Anne Hathaway. They had three children including a set of twins. As a young man he was either a schoolteacher or an apprentice to a butcher.

The first known reference to Shakespeare as an actor and playwright was in 1592. Robert Greene, a well-known poet and playwright, wrote a pamphlet in which he called William an "upstart crow." From 1590 through 1592, three of Shakespeare's plays were performed. Soon after, the theatres were closed due to the plague that decimated much of the English population. Shakespeare continued writing poems and plays. He became known and respected as a great poet.

With the money he earned from his acting and writing, he was part-owner of one of the most popular acting companies in England. He presented his plays at the courts of Queen Elizabeth I and King James I. He also bought the second largest home in Stratford but lived most of his life in London. His acting company was responsible for the establishment of the Globe Theater built in 1599. It was destroyed by fire in 1613. A second Globe Theatre was built on the same site in 1614 and closed in 1644.

In the early 1600s, 152 of Shakespeare's sonnets were published. *Sonnet 18* is considered to be the most famous. He wrote 38 plays. His most famous are *Hamlet, Macbeth, Julius Caesar, The Tempest, Henry IV, King Lear, and Romeo and Juliet.* Shakespeare is recognized as the greatest of all English playwrights.

Sonnet 18
by William Shakespeare

Shall I compare thee to a summer's day?
Thou art more lovely and more temperate:
Rough winds do shake the darling buds of May,
And summer's lease hath all too short a date:
Sometime too hot the eye of heaven shines,
And often is his gold complexion dimm'd;
And every fair from fair sometime declines,
By chance or nature's changing course untrimm'd;
But thy eternal summer shall not fade
Nor lose possession of that fair thou owest;
Nor shall Death brag thou wander'st in his shade,
When in eternal lines to time thou growest:
So long as men can breathe or eyes can see,
So long lives this and this gives life to thee.

DECEMBER LEARNING STANDARDS

Common Core Math

3.MD.A.1 – Tell and write time to the nearest minute and measure time intervals in minutes. Solve word problems involving addition and subtraction of time intervals in minutes, e.g., by representing the problem on a number line diagram.	Minute to Win It
4.OA.A3 – Solve multistep word problems posed with whole numbers and having whole-number answers using the four operations, including problems in which remainders must be interpreted.	Shopping for Holiday Parties
5.NBT.B.7 – Add, subtract, multiply, and divide decimals to hundredths, using concrete models or drawings and strategies based on place value, properties of operations, and/or the relationship between addition and subtraction; relate the strategy to a written method and explain the reasoning used.	Shopping for Holiday Parties

Common Core Language Arts – Literature

RL.3.1 – Ask and answer questions to demonstrate understanding of a text, referring explicitly to the text as the basis for the answers.	*Auld Lang Syne*
4RL.1 – Refer to details and examples in a text explaining what the text says explicitly and when drawing inferences from the text.	*Little Tree*
W.5.3.D – Use concrete words and phrases and sensory details to convey experiences and events precisely.	Winter Haikus
WHST.6-8.9 – Draw evidence from informational texts to support analysis, reflection, and research.	*O! why was I born with a different face?*

Common Core Language Arts – Writing

W.3.5 – With guidance and support from peers and adults develop and strengthen writing as needed by planning, revising and editing.	Winter Haikus
W.4.1.C – Link opinion and reasons using words and phrases.	*A Song for New Years Eve*
5W.5.6 – With some guidance and support from adults, use technology, including the Internet, to produce and publish writing as well as to interact and collaborate with others.	*Auld Lang Syne*
SL.5.1.C – Pose and respond to specific questions by making comments that contribute to the discussion and elaborate on the remarks of others.	*Holidays*

DECEMBER LEARNING STANDARDS

ISTE Technology Standards 2016

1a – Articulate and set personal learning goals, develop strategies leveraging technology to achieve them and reflect on the learning process itself to improve learning outcomes.	Festive December
3d – Students build knowledge by actively exploring real-world issues and problems, developing ideas and theories and pursuing answers and solutions.	National Mutt Day
4a – Students exhibit a tolerance for ambiguity, perseverance and the capacity to work with open-ended problems.	Shopping for Holiday Parties.
6a – Students choose the appropriate platforms and tools for meeting the desired objectives of their creation or communication.	Stationery Design
6d – Students publish or present content that customizes the message and medium for their intended audiences.	Festive December
7b – Students use collaborative technologies to work with others, including peers, experts or community members, to examine issues and problems from multiple viewpoints.	Shopping for Holiday Parties

NGSS and ETS1 Science and Engineering Standards 2016

3 - PS2 – Plan and conduct an investigation to provide evidence of the effects of balanced and unbalanced forces on the motion of an object.	One Minute Drop
5 -PS1-3 – Make observations and measurements to identify materials based on their properties.	Invisible Ink
MS-PS1-2 – Analyze and interpret data on the properties of substances before and after the substances interact to determine if a chemical reaction has occurred.	Invisible Ink
NGSS.MS-PS2-2 – Plan an investigation to provide evidence that the change in an object's motion depends on the sum of the forces on the object and the mass of the object.	One Minute Drop
NGSS 3-5-ETS1-1 – Define a simple design problem reflecting a need or want that includes specified criteria for success and constraints on materials, time or cost.	Gumdrop Bridge
NGSS MS-ETS1-2 – Evaluate completing design solutions using a systematic process to determine how well they meet the material and constraints of the problem.	Gumdrop Bridge

JANUARY LEARNING STANDARDS

Common Core Math

4.MD.A.2 – Use the four operations to solve word problems involving distances, intervals of time, liquid volumes, masses of objects, and money, including problems involving simple fractions or decimals, and problems that require expressing measurements given in a larger unit in terms of a smaller unit.	Milestone Math
4.OA.A3 – Solve multistep word problems posed with whole numbers and having whole-number answers using the four operations, including problems in which remainders must be interpreted.	Milestone Math
5.NF.B.4 –Apply and extend previous understandings of multiplication to multiply a fraction or whole number by a fraction.	Calendar Challenge
5.NF.B.6 – Solve real world problems involving multiplication of fractions and mixed numbers, e.g., by using visual fraction models or equations to represent the problem.	Calendar Challenge

Common Core Language Arts – Literature

RL.3.1 – Ask and answer questions to demonstrate understanding of a text, referring explicitly to the text as the basis for the answers.	*Song of Myself*
RL 4.2 – Determine a theme of a story, drama, or poem from details in the text; summarize the text.	*My Country 'Tis of Thee*
R.L 5.4 – Determine the meaning of words and phrases as they are used in a text, including figurative language such as metaphors and similes.	*Hold Fast to Dreams*
RL.6.4 – Determine the meaning of words and phrases as they are used in a text, including figurative and connotative meanings; analyze the impact of a specific word choice on meaning and tone.	*New Year*

Common Core Language Arts – Writing

W.3.4 – With guidance and support from adults, produce writing in which the development and organization are appropriate to task and purpose.	*Song of Myself*
W.4.2.D – Use precise language and domain-specific vocabulary to inform about or explain the topic.	*Hold Fast to Dreams*
W.5.6 – With some guidance and support from adults, use technology, including the Internet, to produce and publish writing as well as to interact and collaborate with others.	*My Coutry 'Tis of Thee*
SL.5.1.C – Pose and respond to specific questions by making comments that contribute to the discussion and elaborate on the remarks of others.	*Thanksgiving*

January LEARNING STANDARDS

ISTE Technology Standards 2016

1d – Students understand the fundamental concepts of technology operations, demonstrate the ability to choose, use and troubleshoot current technologies and are able to transfer their knowledge to explore emerging technologies.	Photography for A New Year Calendar
3a – Students plan and employ effective research strategies to locate information and other resources for their intellectual or creative pursuits.	Presenting Dr. Martin Luther King, Jr.
3c – Students evaluate and select information sources and digital tools based on the appropriateness to specific tasks.	Presenting Dr. Martin Luther King, Jr.
4a – Students exhibit a tolerance for ambiguity, perseverance and the capacity to work with open-ended problems.	January 18 – Thesaurus Day
6a –Students choose the appropriate platforms and tools for meeting the desired objectives of their creation or communication.	To Life
6d – Students publish or present content that customizes the message and medium for their intended audiences.	To Life
7b – Students use collaborative technologies to work with others, including peers, experts or community members, to examine issues and problems from multiple viewpoints.	Thank You Solar Advocates

NGSS and ETS1 Science and Engineering Standards 2015

3-5ETS1-2 – Generate and compare multiple possible solutions to a problem based on how well each is likely to meet the criteria and constraints of the problem.	Celebrating Laughter Scientifically
5-ESS3-1. Obtain and combine information about ways individual communities use science ideas to protect the Earth's resources and environment.	Thank You Solar Scientists
ETS1-4 – A solution needs to be tested, and then modified on the basis of the test results, in order to improve it.	Assembly Line Thank-You Notes
4-PS3-4 – Apply scientific ideas to design, test, and refine a device that converts energy from one form to another.	Thank You Solar Scientists
MS-ETS1-2 – There are systematic processes for evaluating solutions with respect to how well they meet the criteria and constraints.	New Year's Mandalas
NGSS MS-PS2-2 – Plan an investigation to provide evidence that the change in an object's motion depends on the sum of the forces on the object and the mass of the object.	One Minute Drop
NGSS MS-ETS1-2 – Evaluate completing design solutions using a systematic process to determine how well they meet the material and constraints of the problem.	Assembly Line Thank-You Notes

FEBRUARY LEARNING STANDARDS

Common Core Math

MP1 – Make sense of problems and persevere in solving them.	Mancala Game
MP8 – Look for and express regularity in repeated reasoning.	Mancala Game
3.NF.A.3.B – Recognize and generate simple equivalent fractions, e.g., 1/2 = 2/4, 4/6 = 2/3.	Math Memory Matching Game
4.OA.A.1 – Interpret a multiplication equation as a comparison, e.g., interpret 35 = 5 × 7 as a statement that 35 is 5 times as many as 7 and 7 times as many as 5. Represent verbal statements of multiplicative comparisons as multiplication equations.	Math Memory Matching Game

Common Core Language Arts – Literature

RL.3.1 – Ask and answer questions to demonstrate understanding of a text, referring explicitly to the text as the basis for the answers.	*This Land Is Your Land*
RL.42 – Determine a theme of a story, drama, or poem from details in the text, including how characters in a story or drama respond to challenges or how the speaker in a poem reflects upon a topic; summarize the text.	*We Wear the Mask*
RL.5.3 – Compare and contrast two or more characters, settings, or events in a story or drama, drawing on specific details in the text.	excerpt from *The People, Yes*
RL.6.4 – Determine the meaning of words and phrases as they are used in a text, including figurative and connotative meanings; analyze the impact of a specific word choice on meaning and tone.	*Sonnet 18*

Common Core Language Arts – Writing

W.3.4 – With guidance and support from adults, produce writing in which the development and organization are appropriate to task and purpose.	*A Red, Red Rose*
W.4.4 – Produce clear and coherent writing in which the development and organization are appropriate to task, purpose, and audience.	*Of Old Sat Freedom on the Heights*
W.4.9 – Draw evidence from literary or informational texts to support analysis, reflection, and research.	excerpt from *The People, Yes*

Common Core Language Arts – Speaking and Listening

SL.4.1.D – Review the key ideas expressed and explain their own ideas and understanding in light of the discussion.	*Sonnet 18*
SL.5.1.C – Pose and respond to specific questions by making comments that contribute to the discussion and elaborate on the remarks of others.	*We Wear the Mask*

FEBRUARY LEARNING STANDARDS

ISTE Technology Standards 2016

3a – Students plan and employ effective research strategies to locate information and other resources for their intellectual or creative pursuits.	From Slave to Soldier Civil War Posters
3c – Students evaluate and select information sources and digital tools based on the appropriateness to specific tasks.	Little-Known Presidential Facts Mosaic
4a – Students exhibit a tolerance for ambiguity, perseverance and the capacity to work with open-ended problems.	From Slave to Soldier Civil War Posters
6a –Students choose the appropriate platforms and tools for meeting the desired objectives of their creation or communication.	February 22 – George Washington's Birthday
6d – Students publish or present content that customizes the message and medium for their intended audiences.	February 20 – Metropolitan Museum of Art Opening
7b – Students use collaborative technologies to work with others, including peers, experts or community members, to examine issues and problems from multiple viewpoints.	From Slave to Soldier Civil War Posters

NGSS and ETS1 Science and Engineering Standards 2016

ETSI1-1 – Define a simple design problem reflecting a need or want that that includes specified criteria for success and constraints on materials time and cost.	We Make the Mask
3PS2-1 – Plan and conduct an investigation to provide evidence of the effect of balanced and unbalanced forces on motion.	Lincoln Pennies – Buoyancy, Density and Displacement
3PS2-2 – Make observations and/or measurements of an object's motion to provide evidence that a pattern can be used to predict future motion.	Lincoln Pennies – Buoyancy, Density and Displacement
NGSS MS-ETS1-2 Evaluate completing design solutions using a systematic process to determine how well they meet the material and constraints of the problem.	Food Engineers
3-5-ETS1-2 – Engineering Design Generate and compare multiple possible solutions to a problem based on how well each is likely to meet the criteria and constraints of the problem.	Food Engineers
Grades 3 – 5 – Define a problem using criteria for success and constraints or limits of possible solutions.	Presidential Graphology
MS-ETS1-2 – There are systematic processes for evaluating solutions with respect to how well they meet the criteria and constraints.	Presidential Graphology
4-PS3-3 Energy – Ask questions and predict outcomes about the changes in energy that occur when objects collide.	February 18 – National Battery Day

About Us

GARY CARNOW has been a classroom teacher, administrator, author and educational consultant. Dr. Carnow specializes in administrative and instructional technologies, grants and funding procurement, instructional program development, emerging technologies, makerspaces and 3D printing. He has consulted for major hardware and software computer companies and has written extensively for Tech&Learning magazine. He was one of the first educators to provide content for AOL and the Scholastic Network. Beverly and Gary have written educational materials together for over twenty-five years.

BEVERLY ELLMAN is an educator who has enjoyed wearing many different hats. She has been a classroom teacher, an author of educational publications and an educational product developer. She has enjoyed watching the enthusiasm, energy, and creativity sparked in students as they experience learning and master STEM content. She has co-taught several classes which combined poetry and multimedia through UCLA extension with Joyce Koff. In addition, Joyce and Beverly have worked together presenting educational workshops to various elementary and middle school teachers.

JOYCE KOFF is a poet and a teacher. Her work has been published in numerous poetry journals and she has taught in elementary and middle schools in her self-created program. Joyce makes the reading, understanding and writing of poetry accessible to all students and these methods are applied in this book. Joyce has also conducted classes at UCLA demonstrating to teachers how valuable and rewarding the teaching of hands-on poetry can be. As the resident poet at Coeur d'Alene Elementary School in Venice, California, she taught poetry for over 25 years and was part of the art's team that was awarded the prestigious Los Angeles Music Center's Bravo Award.

SIAN BOWMAN has never lost the giddy excitement she experienced as child when drawing and painting. After graduating from Aberystwyth University with a Masters in Fine Art, specializing in children's book illustration, she started freelancing as an illustrator. She is in her element working on picture books and educational books for children. She finds inspiration for her characters in walking her wonderful, cheeky whippet, Jet, through the countryside of Mid Wales, where her imagination can wander. You can learn more about Sian at sianbowman.com.

Notes

37399477R00094

Made in the USA
Middletown, DE
27 November 2016